T0149326

# THE MUSTARD SEED COUNSELING

## EXPERIENCE GOD'S EMPOWERING PRESENCE IN BIBLICAL COUNSELING

IBRAHIM YOUSSEF, PH.D.

authorHOUSE®

*AuthorHouse™*
*1663 Liberty Drive*
*Bloomington, IN 47403*
*www.authorhouse.com*
*Phone: 1 (800) 839-8640*

*© 2016 Ibrahim Youssef, Ph.D. All rights reserved.*

*No part of this book may be reproduced, stored in a retrieval system, or transmitted by any means without the written permission of the author.*

*Published by AuthorHouse 03/24/2016*

*ISBN: 978-1-5049-8416-4 (sc)*
*ISBN: 978-1-5049-8415-7 (hc)*
*ISBN: 978-1-5049-8414-0 (e)*

*Library of Congress Control Number: 2016903709*

*Print information available on the last page.*

*Any people depicted in stock imagery provided by Thinkstock are models, and such images are being used for illustrative purposes only. Certain stock imagery © Thinkstock.*

*This book is printed on acid-free paper.*

*Because of the dynamic nature of the Internet, any web addresses or links contained in this book may have changed since publication and may no longer be valid. The views expressed in this work are solely those of the author and do not necessarily reflect the views of the publisher, and the publisher hereby disclaims any responsibility for them.*

*Scriptural quotations, unless otherwise stated, are from the New King James Version. Thomas Nelson Inc, 1982.*

*Dedication*
*To Pastor Daniel of Egypt, my brother in law, who does not only know the*
*Word but also he lives the Word*

# Contents

# LISTS OF ILLISTRATIONS

# PREFACE

This book is an invaluable resource for those who want to understand the role of the Holy Spirit especially His fruit and charismatic gifts in biblical counselling. It was originally the dissertation of my Ph.D degree in biblical counselling, Trinity College, Newburgh, Indiana USA.

It takes the reader to a journey from Jay Adams who rediscovered biblical counselling when he published his first book of Competent to Counsel (CtC) in 1970, and how he appreciated the crucial role of the Holy Spirit in his model which he named it Neuthetic Counselling, to the charismatic professor, Dr Gordon Fee and how he enriches our understanding of the Holy Spirit when he examines, in a scholarly way, His fruit and His charismatic gifts. Then we stop at Larry Crabb, the prominent Christian psychologist who tries to make his integration model of secular psychology and Christian faith universal for biblically counselling Christians and non Christians. Unfortunately his model of biblical counselling comes up dry without the Water of the Holy Spirit. Finally, Colin Dye the famous charismatic scholar and the senior pastor of the London City church, UK, who tries to adopt Crabb's integration model. However that does not prevent him from acknowledging the role of the Holy Spirit in biblical counselling, albeit he does not mention that in his core adopted model.

Then I have developed my model of "Mustard Seed of Biblical Counselling." The uniqueness of this model is that it starts with evangelism, referring back to Jay Adams' recommendation, passing through the fruit and the charismatic gifts of the Holy Spirit and ends with glorifying and serving the Lord for His great work that He has been doing in us as believers in our journey in the wildness of this fallen world with all its difficulties and problems.

I pray that this book makes a difference to the readers. First of all, it is to change their lives when they meet and have relationship with the Lord Jesus like what He has done in my life, without Him, there would be no hope either in this world or in the eternity, and indeed there would be no effective biblical counselling. Second, it is to introduce biblical counselling which recently, has attracted growing interest in the UK and worldwide.

Ibrahim Youssef Ph.D
Dorchester UK February 2016

# ACKNOWLEDGMENTS

First of all, I thank God in the Person of the Holy Spirit who gave me the strength and ideas to complete this work. I am deeply grateful to Dr Elbert E Elliott, the Committee Chair, for continuous guidance, indispensable advice, and encouragement to fulfill this work. I thank AuthorHouse staff who designed and published the book.

I awe thanks also to Dr Howard Eyrich my tutor during my study of the Master degree at Trinity whom I learned the basic principles of biblical counseling either from his online lectures or from his book ,"Curing the Heart," and other assigned books of biblical counseling.

I thank the staff at the Trinity College of the Bible, and Theological Seminary for their help and support, especially Sheryle Knight, while working through this project. I thank also Richard Dunkley from Storehouse Pentecostal Church of Dorchester for his encouragement and his comment on the draft. I also thank my Bible study group at the United Church in Dorchester, UK, especially Alison Pople and Pat Bolton who kindly read the draft and made their comments.

I am grateful to Mrs. Bella Blanchard, my English Language teacher, for reviewing the rough draft to appear without grammatical/spelling mistakes and lastly my family, my wife Salwa, and my daughter Joyce for their support during my study for the Ph.D degree.

# ABSTRACT

Jay Adams, the founder of the Nouthetic Biblical Counselling that depends on the confrontation of sin as the corner stone of change, declares that biblical counsellors cannot counsel the unbelievers in the biblical sense of the word (changing them, sanctifying them through the work of the Holy Spirit, as His Word is ministered to their hearts), so long as they remain unbelievers. They need the regeneration work of the Holy Spirit and then, they can be counselled by putting off the works of the flesh (Galatians 5:19-21) and putting on the fruit of the Spirit (Galatians 5:22-23). The Holy Spirit empowers them while they pursue His luscious fruit and that might be all they need from biblical counselling.

Golden Fee points out that we live in a time (postmodern period), similar to the Greco-roman time when the Church of Jesus Christ started at the day of Pentecost. The message of the Gospel was spread across the whole ancient world by the apostles. Their success relied not only on the proclamation of our Lord Jesus who died for our sins on the Cross and rose from the dead, but also they were empowered by God's presence of the Holy Spirit. Fee disagrees with Adams on the issue that the charismatic gifts of the Spirit, as recorded in 1 Corinthians 12:1-11, have ceased. Fee declares that they are relevant today as at the day of Pentecost. The Holy Spirit still works in the believers now powerfully with miracles and wonders as we come nearer to the end of the age, waiting for the second coming of the Lord Jesus Christ our redeemer.

Colin Dye, the charismatic and the senior pastor of the largest Pentecostal church in Europe (London City Church, KT, UK) planned to publish three counselling manuals corresponding to three counselling levels to establish a counselling ministry in the Church. However, in doing that, he adopted Larry Crabb's model of integration of Christian faith with secular psychology. In his first manual, he suggests that all church members should be level I counsellors, in the sense that they encourage and support other members passing through difficulties or problems. Although the original Crabb's model ignores completely the role of the Holy Spirit, that does not prevent Dye from saying that the encouragers should have the fruit of the Spirit of Galatians 5, especially joy and love. In his second manual, Dye develops a model similar to Crabb's with some modification. In the introduction of his model, he points out that the Holy Spirit is needed to empower the change required, especially His gifts of revelation: the word of wisdom, the word of knowledge, and prophecy. Dye does not publish the third manual as he planned; the reason for that is not known.

In the final chapter of this study, I have developed a counselling model, The Mustard Seed Counselling, based entirely on the fruit and the charismatic gifts of the Spirit, as well as the Word of God. That highlights the crucial role of the Holy Spirit in biblical counselling, opening the door for future studies to explore this area in biblical counselling which is currently ignored.

## Chapter One

# INTRODUCTION

*So Jesus said to them, "Because of your unbelief; for assuredly,*
*I say to you, if you have faith as a Mustard Seed, you will say*
*to this mountain, 'Move from here to there,' and it will move;*
*and nothing will be impossible for you."*

Mathew 17:20

In February 2013, CCEF /USA (Christian Counseling Education Foundation)[1] launched CCEF/UK by a conference entitled, "Changing Hearts, Applying the Bible to Everyday Life," at the Central Hall, Westminster in London. The two main speakers were Dr David Powlison[2]

---

[1] CCEF, based in Philadelphia USA, has been providing a Christian counselling ministry for over 40 years. With a passion for personal change centred in the person of Christ, they constantly revisit the question, "How do the riches of the Gospel impact our own lives and our efforts to help others?"

[2] Is a faculty member at CCEF and Senior Editor of the Journal of Biblical counselling (JBC). He has been counselling for over thirty years and has written numerous articles and books on biblical counselling and on the relationship between faith and psychology.

and Time Lane³, from CCEF /USA. At the end of the conference, they were asked if it would be appropriate to biblically counsel an unbeliever. There was a debate between the two. The end result was that they believed it would be possible with the hope that during the counseling sessions, the counselee would come to a decision and accept Jesus as the Savior, and thus he would have benefited from biblical counseling and they could have won a soul for the kingdom of God.

However, I have some reservations on this point. The Holy Spirit, the concern of this study, does not dwell in unbelievers, and by the time the counselee accepts Jesus as the Savior, he would not be spiritually mature enough to appreciate the crucial role of the Holy Spirit as God's empowering presence in the biblical counseling.

**Jay Adams**⁴ (1973)⁵ confirmed that biblical counseling should be for believers only. He says that, in truly biblical counseling, the counselor and the counselee meet in the name of Jesus Christ. They should expect the very presence of Christ as the Counselor-in-charge, according to the Scripture, when Jesus says, "For where two or three are gathered together in my name, I am in the midst of them."⁶

---

³ Is president and faculty member at CCEF and has been counselling for more than 25 years. He wrote many books include, "How people change" Also he served as a pastor for ten years.

⁴ Jay Adams is the former director of advanced studies and professor of practical theology at Westminster Theological Seminary and a retired pastor. He is well-known by many scholars as the father of the current biblical counselling movement. He founded and had been the dean of Christian Counselling Education Foundation CCEF, before he retired to dedicate himself to writing and teaching. He has written around 50 books on pastoral ministry and biblical counselling including, Competent to Counsel, Christian Counselling Manual, and others. He currently teaches online at www.nouthetic.org.

⁵ Jay Adams, *The Christian Counsellor's Manual: The Practice of Nouthetic Counselling* (Grand Rapids, MI Zondervan, 1973),4.

⁶ Mathew 18:20. This verse closely follows the reconciliation passage (Mathew 18:15-17) and is indeed, part of it.

Adams continues to explain that the Holy Spirit is the Principal Person.[7] He points to what Jesus says before leaving His disciples, "And I will send another (allos) Helper (parakeltos), that may abide with you forever."[8] The Greek word "*allos*" is translated literally as "another of the same kind." "Parakeltos" in Greek can also be translated to advocate, counselor, and intercessor. John MacArthur (2005),also highlights this issue.[9]

Adams explains further by saying, when Jesus was on earth, He was God appearing in flesh, similar to us in everything except without sin. He was limited to time and place. So as He explained to His disciples later, that it was for their benefit that He had to depart as He said in John 16-7, "Nevertheless I tell you the truth, it is to your advantage that I go away; for if I do not go away, the Helper will not come to you; but if I depart, I will send Him to you."

Because the Holy Spirit, who has come, is not limited to time or place, He, for example, can be at the counseling sessions in China and in the USA at the same time. He is the Spirit of Truth and He is indeed the Spirit of holiness, and the source of holiness. The holiness of God's people results from their sanctification by the Holy Spirit. Sanctification is the ultimate goal of biblical counseling. To sum up, Christians cannot counsel or be counseled biblically without the Holy Spirit.

However, Adams disagrees with the other two scholars, Gordon Fee and Colin Dye, on two issues. First, he says that the Holy Spirit does not dwell in the believers. The Holy Spirit dwells in the Church as the body of Christ only. However, for the believers, the Spirit works through the Bible. We read and understand the Scripture effectively through the Holy Spirit, and then live in obedience to His truth. Second, all Christians benefit from

---

[7] Jay Adams' manual, 5-8.

[8] John 14:16.

[9] John MacArthur, *Counseling: How to Counsel Biblically* (Nashville: Thomas Nelson,2005), 80-81.

His counsel, but the Holy Spirit counseled the apostles in a unique way, enabling them to remember the work of Jesus and the revelations written in the Bible. However, the supernatural charismatic gifts, described in 1 Corinthian 12-14, the apostles had, were *ceased* [10]by the close of the New Testament canon.

**Gordon Fee**[11] (1996) writes that we live in what he calls a "postmodern world,"[12] where the Church is regularly viewed as irrelevant at best and Neanderthal[13] at worst. The Holy Spirit, despite our profession of faith in our creeds, hymns and lip service has largely been marginalized both in the halls of learning, and in the life of the Church. But there is reason for hope, as Fee explains. Our contemporary post-modernism era looks much like the culture of the Greco-Roman world into which the Gospel first appeared some two thousand years ago. The secret to the success of the early believers lay in two factors. First, upon the good news, this was centered on the life, death, and resurrection of Jesus. Jesus, Immanuel, had come, brought both revelation and the character of God to our fallen world. John 14:9, the Lord Jesus says, "Have you been with me for so long and don't know who I am? The one who has seen me has seen the Father." Jesus is our redeemer from our tragic fall, as written in Matth1:21, "You shall call his name Yeshua, for He will save his people from their sins." The second reason for their success laid in *their experienced the Spirit who*

---

[10] Although Adams does not mention literary that the charismatic gifts of 1 Corinthian 12-14 had ceased, I understand that when he mentions only the gifts of ministry not the charismatic gifts. This issue will be explained fully later in this study.

[11] Gordon Fee is professor emeritus of New Testament at Regent College Vancouver. He is the author of numerous books, including New Testament Exegesis, God's Empowering Presence, Pauline Christology, and several commentaries.

[12] Gordon D Fee, *Paul the Spirit, and the people of God* (Grand Rapids, MI: Baker Academic Publication, 1996) pp xiii-xv.

[13] An organisation holding very old fashioned views (paperback, Oxford English dictionary, page 562)

*made the work of Christ an effective reality in their lives, thus giving them a radical alternative within their culture.*

To explain Fee's second reason for the early believers' success in their Greco-Roman culture, I quote here what is written in Acts 1:3-8. The Apostle Luke records that the Lord Jesus was with his disciples, 40 days after His resurrection. The disciples had more than three years of intensive teaching from the Lord Himself. They saw with their own eyes, the Lord's resurrection from the dead and He was now with them talking. There was nothing preventing them from preaching the Gospel, the good news. However, Jesus instructed them, "not depart from Jerusalem, and you should wait for the promise of the Father, because you *shall receive power when the Holy Spirit has come to you.*"

Although Fee does not examine biblical counseling in his books, the above same principles should be applied. We need, as counselors and counselees, to fully appreciate the power of the Holy Spirit to make our counseling sessions more effective in our postmodern world. We need to stop paying lip service to the Spirit and to recapture the Apostle Paul's perspective: the Holy Spirit is the experienced empowering return of God's own personal presence in and among us. The good news is that we do not have to wait. The Holy Spirit already dwells in us as believers.

**Colin Dye**[14] has developed his model of biblical counseling influenced by Larry Crabb's model of integration of Christian faith with secular psychology.[15] He planned to write three counseling manuals, each corresponding to the three counseling levels suggested by Crabb, to establish a counseling service in the church. However, he wrote and

---

[14] Colin Dye is senior pastor of Kensington Temple and leader of London City Church UK. He Has authored over 30 books, covering subjects as prayer, ministry of the Holy Spirit, Church Growth and Biblical Counselling. He is the head and lecturer of the IBIOL, The International Bible Institute of London UK.

[15] He planned to write three counselling manuals corresponding to the three counselling levels suggested by Larry Crabb: Level 1: Encouragement. Level 2:Exhortation. Level 3: Enlightenment. He wrote the first two but the third one was not written.

published only two of them. The third manual has never come to light. The fruit and the charismatic gifts of the Holy Spirit in these manuals will be examined in Dye's chapter of this study. However, it is worth looking at his view on the Holy Spirit's fruit and the charismatic gifts from his other books he wrote on this topic.

In his book (2007) titled "Knowing the Spirit," he points out that the Holy Spirit is known to make a difference. We may see Him as a hurricane wind or another person like the Lord Jesus; we have to recognize that He is always bringing a decisive change. This change is through His fruit and the gifts He provides to believers.

## The Purity of the Spirit[16]

In the New Testament, all believers are called "saints." The word "saints" is translated from the Greek word "hagios" meaning they are devoted to God. There are many other words in the Greek language with similar meanings like " hieros" or "semnos." But "hagios" primarily describes the nature of the Holy Spirit applied to the believers. This means that holiness is not something we aspire to or attain; rather it is a state into which God, in his grace, has called us and in which we live. The *fruit* of the Spirit in us is that He transforms our moral and spiritual character so that our lives begin to reflect the standing we already have in God's sight. In other words, the Holy Spirit brings about "sanctification" in us. However, one cannot have this fruit automatically. When we receive the Spirit in salvation, we start walking in the Spirit and begin allowing Him to remake us in Christ's image. In Galatians 5, there is tension between the works of the flesh and the fruit of the Spirit. However, the Holy Spirit gives us power to overcome the works of the flesh in order to enjoy the fruit and the purity of the Spirit.

---

[16] Colin Dye, *Knowing the Spirit* (London: Kensington Temple Publication,2007), pp 83-93

Dye continues to say that purity here is the purity from sin. Romans 3:9 teaches us that unsaved human beings are trapped in the power of sin, and Romans 7:20-23 shows that sin exists in those who have been born again. While some believe that Romans 7 is dealing with the experience of unbelievers, Paul's description of the struggle with indwelling sin shows that it is the experience of every believer. However the Spirit is God's agent of purity. He makes us "born again." He provides us with the "new heart" which creates the possibility, which did not previously exist, of living in purity and obeying God's commandments. He shapes our lives and regenerates us. He enables us to receive the very nature of Christ and to become more and more like Him throughout our earthly lives.

## The Spiritual Gifts

Dye (2007)[17] talks about the charismatic gifts. The Greek word *charisma* means "gifts of grace." Dye says there are more gifts than those mentioned in 1 Corinthians 12:1-11, such as the ones mentioned for example in Ephesians 4:8-11 and Romans 12:6-8, but the nine gifts of 1 Corinthians 12, are entirely new, according to Dye.

We, as believers, are channels for the Spirit's attributes,[18] not a reservoir containing them. The gifts' goal is to direct others to glorify Christ.[19] Dye describes these nine gifts as follows:

1. A word of Wisdom: a supernatural skill to resolve or assist a situation. It is not gained through experience or training, but by glimpsing the Spirit's wisdom

---

[17] Colin Dye, *Knowing the Spirit* (London: Kensington Temple Publication, 2007) pp98-101.

[18] In the sense that we deliver the gifts for the benefit of others. This will be explained later in Dye's chapter.

[19] In the sense that when a person is healed, he/she should glorify the Lord not the person who delivers this gift.

2. A word of knowledge: the supernatural revelation of facts about a person or situation. We do not learn it naturally, we see a fragment of the Spirit's knowledge

3. Gifts of healing: Knowledge to know, whom, how and when God wants to heal a person for the glory of God. It is not a permanent gift to possess, as Dye explains

4. Faith: it is to trust God to do something seemingly impossible

5. Miracles: the supernatural operation of miraculous powers through a person, by the Spirit, when God chooses to intervene in the natural order

6. Prophecy: a supernatural receiving from the Spirit of a message from God for an individual or group of people

7. Discerning of spirits: the supernatural insight from the Spirit which identifies motivating spirits behind a word or an action of an individual

8. Different kinds of tongues: the Spirit-given words to pray to God in a language which has not been learnt. This frees us to pray with the Spirit instead of the mind

9. Interpretation or explanation of tongues: the supernatural revelation from the Spirit of the gist of what someone has prayed in tongues.

The Holy Spirit wants us to ask for and pursue these gifts and also to make very good use of them. The focus must be to build up and serve others through these gifts.

In this context, Fee (1996)[20] points out that, the broad spectrum of phenomena are best grouped under the three natural headings hinted at 1 Corinthian 12:4-6: service, miracles, and inspired utterances.

---

[20] Gordon Fee's, *Paul, the Spirit and the People of God* (Grand Rapids, MI:BakerAcademic Publicaios,1996) pp 163-178

**Forms of Service,** Items listed include, 1 Corinthians 12:28: "helpful deeds," and "guidance." Also Romans 12:7-8 "serving," "giving," and "caring." In a broad sense, these are the Spirit activities within the Church. To include these as charismatic makes the category useless.

**The Miraculous:** Included here, are three items from 1 Corinthians 12:9-10, "faith," "gifts of healings," and "workings of miracles." The recurrence in 13:2 makes certain, "faith" is referring to the supernatural faith that can "move mountains." For the "gifts of healing," Paul means the healing of the physical body. In Paul's theology, the healings of mind and spirit occur at conversion. The "workings of miracles" are all other such phenomena not included in healing.

According to Fee, there are reasons why the "gifts of healing," and the "workings of miracles" are different categories and also they are not permanent.

**Inspired Utterance:** 1 Corinthians 12:8-10: "the message of wisdom,"[21] "the message of Knowledge,"[22] "prophecy," "the discrimination of S/spirits," "tongues," and "the discrimination of tongues." Also in1 Corinthians 14:6 this category includes "teaching," and "revelation,"[23] according to Fee.

Whether the charismatic gifts include the gifts of ministry or not, or whether they are only nine or more than nine, for the interest and the scope of this study, only the nine gifts of the Spirit described in 1 Corinthians 12:1-11 are studied with their benefits in biblical counseling.[24]

---

[21] NKJV = " the word of wisdom."

[22] NKJV = "the word of knowledge."

[23] According to Dye, revelation gifts include word of wisdom, word of knowledge, and prophecy.

[24] According to Dye, charismatic gifts include all the special gifts of the Holy Spirit, However, what are mentioned in 1 Corinthians 12:1-11are special because they are new. For Fee the charismatic gifts are "such as" mentioned in this passage of 1 Corinthians 12.

# An Outline of the Narrative

Chapter two: A literature's review of the fruit and the charismatic gifts of the Holy Spirit from the writings of different theologians, also a review of biblical counseling.

Chapter three: Jay Adams' model of "Nouthetic Counseling" and how he applies the fruit and the gifts of the Holy Spirit in his counseling agenda as evident from his writings

Chapter four: the analysis of the fruit and the gifts of the Holy Spirit in Gordon Fee's books: "Paul the Spirit and the People of God" and "God's Empowering Presence" and the application of the Apostle Paul' theology in biblical counseling.

Chapter five: examines Colin Dye's model of counseling which is adopted from Larry Crabb's model of integration of psychology with the Christian faith, and how he applies the fruit and the charismatic gifts of the Spirit in his model.

Chapter six: the "Mustard Seed" model of biblical counseling that I have developed which is based entirely on the fruit and the charismatic gifts of the Holy Spirit, and on the Scripture as the sole material for counseling.

Chapter seven: the conclusion of the study and final statement.

# Chapter Two

# THE HOLY SPIRIT AND HOW HE EMPOWERS BIBLICAL COUNSELING

Before examining the fruit and the gifts of the Holy Spirit, the biblical counselor should be prepared to answer some basic questions about the Holy Spirit, when he/she is asked by a counselee. For example, who is the Holy Spirit? Is he a person or just a power? How does the Holy Spirit work in the world and in the believers? Also some other questions like, what is meant by the baptism of the Holy Spirit and the filling by the Spirit?

Francis Schaeffer[25], the Swiss scholar finds himself wrestling with a deeply perplexing question. He is tired of not seeing changes in his own spiritual life and others. He then examines his Christian faith from the beginning, and asks, "Does Christianity really make any differences or changes in my life or the life of others?" So he writes his book, "True Spirituality"(30th Anniversary Edition, 2001) as the result of his honest search for answers.

---

[25] A Swiss bible scholar and the founder of L'Abri Fellowship in the Swiss village of Huemoz-sur Ollon. He was a lecturer and pastor. He was regarded as a great prophet of the latter part of the twelfth century . He was God's most powerful voice to both Church and culture.

In his book[26], Schaeffer quotes Romans 6:11, "likewise you also, reckon yourself to be dead indeed to sin, but alive in God in Christ Jesus our Lord." He also quotes Christ saying to His disciples in John 14:18, "I will not leave you orphans; I will come to you." He concludes that the changes required in personality, thoughts, behavior and so forth (which is what biblical counseling all about) should be through the power of the crucified, risen, and glorified Christ, through the *agency*[27] of the Holy Spirit. So according to him, the Holy Spirit works in the believers' hearts as a power to motivate them to change.[28]

Youssef Riad, the Egyptian bible scholar at the Arabic Christian program, "Kolelketab" or "Thru Bible,"[29] explains that the Holy Spirit is a *person* equal to God in character. The Apostle Paul says, in 2 Corinthians 3:17, that, "'The Lord is the Spirit, and where the Spirit of the Lord is, there is liberty." The Lord Jesus says in John 4:24, that, "God is Spirit, and those who worship Him must worship in Spirit and Truth." So the theologians who say that He is just a power, are either ignorant or for a purpose like Jehovah's Witness. God is one in three persons-The Spirit, the Son and the Father. To confirm that the Holy Spirit is a person, the Apostle Luke says in Acts 13:2, "As they ministered to the Lord and fasted, the Holy Spirit *said*, now separate to Me Barnabas and Saul for the work to which I have called." Also, the Holy Spirit has emotions, for example, the Apostle Paul says in Ephesians 4:30, "And do not *grieve* the Holy Spirit of God, by

---

[26] Francis A Schaeffer, *True Spirituality* (Washington DC: Tyndale House Publishers, 2001) pp41-53.

[27] Collins English Dictionary page 11: *agency* means: old-fashioned power or action by which something happens.

[28] Although Schaeffer believes that God is three persons in one, God the Father, The Son, and the Holy Spirit, he restricts the Holy Spirit's role to just a power. Larry Crabb is affected by Schaeffer's writings as he declares that in his book, "Basic Principles of Biblical Counselling"p12.

[29] Youssef Riad, *The study of Galatians* (episode 17, broadcasted on the 21st of May 2015) YouTube.

whom you were sealed for the day of redemption." So if the Holy Spirit is just a power, how could the power talk or be sad?

Other scholars like Samuel Jardine(2010)[30] write that the Holy Spirit is a divine Person, having equality as well as union with the Father and the Son, members of the God-head in the baptismal formula recorded in Mathew 28:19, when the Lord Jesus said that "----baptizing them into the *name* (not in the names) of the Father and of the Son, and of the Holy Spirit."

## The Holy Spirit in the World

Jardine [31] quotes a reading from John 15: 18-25, where the Lord Jesus describes the term "World" as "Cosmos" which suggests an ordered society under a strong and powerful ruler called the Master, the prince of this world. Here is the kingdom of Satan. The World and his master hated the Lord when He was on earth. The same is applied for those who follow Christ now. The World resists the Holy Spirit as it used to resist the Lord Jesus. To understand this enormous transgression, it must be remembered that all Christ's signs and wonders that He did while He was on earth were done through the Holy Spirit.

To understand how the Holy Spirit works in the World, Jardine quotes, John 16:8, when the Lord Jesus says that, "And when He (the Holy Spirit) has come, He will convict the World of sin and of righteousness, and of judgment." Jardine explains this verse by saying that the conviction of sin is the refusal of Christ as the Savior; of righteousness, that Christ is the only sinless person who carried our sins when He died for us on the Cross, and lastly, of judgment of the ruler of the World, Satan, who has

---

[30] Samuel Jardine, *The Work and the Person of the Holy Spirit* (Stanton Drew, Bristol: Seed Publication,2010) pp 11-14

[31] Samuel Jardine, *The Person and the Work of the Holy Spirit*(Stanton Drew, Bristol: Seed Publication,2010) pp 27-33.

been already judged, is waiting to be executed and those who follow him will share his doom.

## The Holy Spirit in the Believer

Jardine[32] writes that the miracle of regeneration (or salvation) is entirely the act of the Spirit, by which He imparts God's life for the soul, thus transferring the new-born from the kingdom of Satan into the kingdom of God. This is quite evident when the Lord Jesus answered Nicodemus, "Most assuredly, I say to you, unless one is born of water (the Word of God) and the Spirit, he cannot enter the kingdom of God" (John 3:5).

Jardine continues to say that, during this miracle of regeneration, the Holy Spirit applies the enlightening, cleansing, and quickening power of the Word of truth into the saved mind. As a sinner trusts the Lord Jesus Christ, the Holy Spirit breathes God's own life into his /her soul who, there and then, becomes a child of God. Friends and families should notice the difference in the new believer's life as the result. The dominated sin will have no power. Christ will become his Master. God's people become his associate. He will obey God's commands. His life and conduct will all change. He will be a new man in Christ. That is why "the miracle of salvation" is the greatest miracle of all.

The Holy Spirit is given to *all new believers immediately and unconditionally.* 1 Cornth.6:19, the Apostle Paul says, "Or do you not know that your body is the temple of the Holy Spirit who is *in you,* whom you have from God, and you are not your own?" There is no such thing as a Christian (a true believer) devoid of the Spirit. There are no empty temples in the economy of grace. The salvation here has referred to its origin in the loving heart of the Father; it has its basis in the redemptive work of

---

[32] Samuel Jardine, *The Person and Work of the Holy Spirit* (Stanton Drew, Bristol: Seed Publication, 2010),pp 35-62

the Son, as well as, it has its eternal security and present enjoyment in the presence of the Holy Spirit.

Jardine then describes the life of the believer when he walks in the Spirit after salvation. He quotes, John 7:36, when the Lord Jesus says, "Who believes in Me, as the Scripture has said, out of his heart will flow rivers of living water."[33] Jardine wonders about the words of the Lord, "As the Scripture said." He may be referring to Ezekiel's vision of water /the Holy Spirit in chapter 47. The water comes down the south of the Altar (suggests the Calvary-cost of redemption). The measured stages are:

a)  Waters to the ankles: walk in the Spirit
b)  Waters to the knees: prayer in the Spirit
c)  Waters to the loins: strength by the Spirit
d)  Waters to swim in: the fullness of the Spirit.

## Spirit Baptism

According to Alban Douglas [34](1966), baptism of the Holy Spirit is a highly controversial issue among evangelists and theologians. The biblical counselor should be prepared to help the counselee to understand, not confuse him/her on this most difficult and complex problem.

According to Fee,[35] traditional churches believe that the Spirit comes to a person (usually when he/she is a baby) through the event of water baptism itself, much like the dove descended on Jesus in the waters of

---

[33] The living water in the Bible refers to the Holy Spirit, as in John 4:14.

[34] Alban Douglas, *One Hundred Bible Lessons* (Manila, Italy: O.M.F Publishers,1966), page 78

[35] Gordon Fee, *Paul, the Spirit and the people of God* (Grand Rapids, MI: BakerAcademic Publications), pp 194-195.

baptism,[36] which is viewed as a model for the later Christening of babies. Fee believes that what happened to Jesus was an exception and should not be taken as a rule. He mentions many verses in the Scripture to support his claim. For example,1 Corinth. 1:14, the Apostle Paul says that, "I thank God that I baptized (with water) none of you except Crispus and Galus." However, the key verse of this issue lies in 1 Corinth. 12:13, as he also says, " For by one Spirit, we were all baptized into one body----." So, if he only baptized two (or a few) with water, how could all the believers have been baptized with one Spirit? So his latter verse means, without confusion, that the Spirit baptism is completely different from water baptism.

However there is another issue that theologians have different opinions about, which is, could the Spirit baptism occur at the time of conversion in one package or on different separate occasions. On the one hand, theologians who support the first view, like Jordine,[37] say that the Holy Spirit unites the new believer with the body of Christ, (the Church) at the moment when the believer is born again at the time of conversion. So, it is once and unrepeatable, which differs from being filled with the Spirit which can happen many times. Fee[38] agrees on this doctrine by saying that for Paul, life in the Spirit begins at conversion. The Pauline images for baptism, death and resurrection and being "clothed to be in Christ," suggest that it is not merely a rite, but the Spirit baptism is part of the package of the whole conversion process. Because immersion was the normal mode of baptism, it provides Paul with a rich metaphor to indicate that the role of baptism is complex.

---

[36] When Jesus was baptised, the Holy Spirit descended in bodily form like a dove upon Him. (Luke 21,22)

[37] Samuel Jardine *The person and Work of the Holy Spirit*, (Stanton Drew, Bristol: Seed Publication,2010), p 56

[38] Gordon Fee *Paul, the Spirit, and the people of God* (Grand Rapids, MI: BakerAcademic Publication) Page 202

On the other hand, there are theologians saying otherwise. They support the separation of the two events (conversion and Spirit baptism). R.T Kendall[39] is an example. He first defines baptism in general as one to be immersed and drenched. So, it is a conscious event unlike the conversion which is unconscious one. His view is based on Acts 8. The people of Samaritan were converted when they heard Philip's preaching with signs and wonders in verse 7, and they were even water baptized. However they waited for Peter Simon, and the other apostles to come down from Jerusalem to lay hands on them to receive the Holy Spirit (Verse 17). The same happened to Saul of Tarsus. He was already converted on the route to Damascus, and yet Ananias was sent to him that he might, "see again and be filled (or baptized) with the Holy Spirit." (Acts 9:17-19). Kendall concludes that the baptism with the Holy Spirit is a *conscious experience* and generally *follows* conversion.

The separation view is also held by Jack Hayford,[40] who confirms that the baptism with the Holy Spirit is a distinct experience available *after* a believer's new birth through faith in Christ as the Savior and the Lord. In other words, it occurs after conversion in a separate event.

Fee[41] solves this issue. He manages, skillfully, to get the two views together, by saying that the experience of the ever-present Spirit, although it starts from conversion by Spirit baptism, can be fanned into flame, and be conscious presence many times in a believer's life. People of God need to be truly people of the Spirit in our present world. However, the quantitative language is strictly avoided when talking about Spirit –filled believers.

---

[39] R.T. Kendall *Holyfire* (Lake Mary, Florida: Charisma House),pp131-138

[40] Jack Hayford, Foreword chapter, *HolyFire*,Kendall,s book, "Holyfire" page xxv

[41] Gordon Fee book, *Paul, the Spirit and the People of God* (Grand Rapids, MI: BakerAcadmic Publications) Page 202

# The filling of the Spirit

Jardine[42] describes two situations in which the filling of the Spirit is needed:

1. An emergency situation needs emergency spiritual power. For example, Acts 6:15, Stephen, when he stood before the Jewish Sanhedrin was *filled with the Spirit.* "And all who sat in the Council, looking steadfastly at him, saw his face as the face of an angel." The Holy Spirit gave him the words and strength to speak before the highest religious Jewish court at that time.

2. Being continually filled with the Spirit makes a believer mature, and gives experience of things that make other believers come to him for advice and guidance on things related to the kingdom of God. For example, Barnabas, in Acts 11.24, "He was a good man, and *full of the Holy Spirit.*" The church at Jerusalem could safely entrust him with the work of investigation called for, when the Gentiles in Antioch were reported to be hearing and receiving the Gospel. In this context, the Apostle Paul says in 2 Tim:1:7, "For God has not given us a spirit of fear, but of power, and of love and of a *sound mind.*" The believer who is filled with the Holy Spirit does not have a confused but a sound mind.

In conclusion, to be filled with the Spirit is to live life to the full, under the control of the un-grieved Spirit.[43]

---

[42] Samuel Jardine, *The Person and Work of the Holy Spirit.*(Stanton Drew, Bristol: Seed Publication), Pp56-62.

[43] Ephesians 4:30: "And do not grieve the Holy Spirit, by whom you were sealed for the day of redemption." Grieve the Holy Spirit is by committing sins but if that happens, the believer quickly repents.

## The Fruit of the Spirit

Jardine[44] records what is written by the Apostle Paul in Galatians 5, about the fruit of the Spirit. The Apostle Paul makes a contrast between the works of the flesh in Galatians 5:19-21, and the fruit of the Spirit, the concern of this study, in Galatians in 5:22-23. It is a great transformation of personality trait and character, from being very bad to being holy and kind.[45] From adultery, fornication, hatred, contentiousness, jealousy, outbursts of wrath, selfishness, dissension, heresy, envy, murder, drunkenness, and revelries----- to love, joy, peace, long-suffering, kindness, goodness, faithfulness, gentleness, and self control which only happens by and through the Holy Spirit.

In this context, Alban Douglas (1966) [46] says that most theologians agree that the fruit of the Spirit as mentioned in Gal. 5:22-23 is the result of the Holy Spirit operating in the new life of the believer. The fruit of the Spirit is spoken of in the singular form signifying the ones of the fruit. The Christian who has been born again in Spirit is not complete until he manifests all the nine graces.

## The Gifts of the Spirit

Douglas continues to say that the gifts of the Spirit mentioned in the Bible are twenty four in total; they are different from the fruit of the Spirit mentioned above. Nine of these gifts are supernatural (the concern of this study) and are stated in 1 Corinth 1-11.[47] The rest are gifts working in the

---

[44] Samuel Jardine, "*The Person and the Work of the Holy Spirit*" (Stanton Drew, Bristol: Seed Publication), pp53-56.

[45] Many Christian converts experience such change that is impossible to happen without the fruit of the Holy Spirit.

[46] Alan Douglas, *One Hundred Bible Lessons* (Manila, Italy: O.M.T Publishers,1966), page 81

[47] The supernatural gifts of 1 Corinthians 1-11 are: word of wisdom, word of knowledge, faith, healing, miraculous powers, prophecy, distinguishing between spirits .speaking in

Church empowering the ministry and evangelism (according to Eph 4:11-16 and Romans 12:6-8).

Herman Riddernos (1997)[48] calls the supernatural gifts "charismata."[49] He adds, although these gifts are given mainly to individual believers, the Apostle Paul directs against individualism that can be strengthened by the diversity of these charismata. Paul talks about love in chapter of 1 Corinthians 13. To tie love with charismata together, these supernatural gifts or charismata are given to individuals to build one another in love and in unity. Without love, even the most excellent charismata count for nothing.[50]

However, there are many theologians who claim that these gifts have ceased. R.T. Kendall[51] calls those "Cessationists." He defines them as those who believe that God on His own "ceased" a long time ago to deal with His people in a supernatural way. He adds, there is a similarity between cessationism and the teaching of deism[52]. Deists believe in one God but could not accept His supernatural gifts of the Spirit. According to them, these gifts are out of the question.

Kendall disagrees with those cessationits by saying that the Holy Spirit still works today, supernaturally, in the same way as he worked at the time of the apostles and the early Church. Hebrews 13:18, says that, "Jesus Christ is the same yesterday, and today and forever." In this context, he recalls Charles Carrin's view in this issue in his booklet, *"On Whose*

---

tongues, and interpretation of tongues.

[48] Herman Ridderbos, *Paul, An Outline of His Theology* (Grand Rapids, MI: Erdmans) pp 295-296.

[49] Origin in Greek, kharisma (in Christian believe) a special gift given by God. Oxford English Dictionary, Paperback page 138.

[50] 1 Corinthians 13:1-3

[51] R.T. Kendall *HolyFire*, (Holy Mary, Florida: Charisma House,2014) pp 107-116

[52] Belief in the existence of an all-powerful creator who does not intervene in the universe, Oxford Dictionary, p216

*Authority? The Removal of Unwanted Scripture.*"[53] Carrin, who had been an ardent cessationist and the pastor of the Primitive Baptist Church in Atlanta, was filled with the Holy Spirit; he was never the same again as he experienced the supernatural gifts especially the speaking in tongues. He faced objection from his own church and as the result, he was forced to resign.

Kendall[54] comments on the above case by saying that the speaking in tongues appears to have a costly implication. He examines the nine gifts of the Spirit mentioned in 1 Corinth. 1-11. He notices that the speaking in tongues is at the bottom of these gifts. He sometimes thinks some church leaders would be willing to drop their theological view that the gifts have ceased, if tongues were not included in the list. Why is that? Was that because it was a stigma-offense in Paul's day? The Scripture does not say that, but certainly it is today. Moreover, as Carrin says, this gift challenges cessationists' pride.

Jen Waters in her article at Washington Times newspaper,[55] records a survey done by a religious education firm about speaking in tongues in Southern Baptist church, USA. The result indicates that half of the Baptist pastors in that region believe that speaking in tongues is a legitimate spiritual gift, ignoring their leaders who have backed the theory that such spiritual gifts,as described in the New Testament, were legitimate only in the early years of the Church. The result shows the on-going debate about the charismatic and Pentecostal movement that, as the writer says, has grown up in the past 100 years.

Fee[56] concludes that whether the "speaking in tongues" in contemporary Pentecostal and charismatic communities is the same in kind as that

---

[53] Charles Carrin Ministries at www.charlecarrin.ministries.com

[54] R.T. Kendall, *HolyFire* (Lake Mary, Florida: Charisma House,2014) pp143-145.

[55] Jen Waters, *Speaking in Tongues,* Washington Times (6/26/2007), p13.

[56] Gordon D Fee, *Paul, the Spirit and the People of God* (Grand Rapids, MI: BakerAcademic Publications, 1996) page 170.

of Pauline churches, there is simply no way to know, however for its practitioners (including myself) it has value similar to that described by Paul.

## An outline of the Charismata of 1 Corinth. 12: 1-11

Referring back, Jardine explained Ezekiel 47. The believer needs to be filled with the Spirit. Before that, he/she should walk, pray and have strength in the Spirit, in stages as previously mentioned, then ask God for the Spirit's gifts. To get a guide for the charismatic gifts, the concern for this study, I include here what Kendall[57] writes about these gifts.

Kendall writes a general comment, which is whereas one might have two or more of these gifts; another person may have only one of them. Also, a gift may flourish only once and never again. Sometimes a gift of the Spirit may reside permanently in a person.

**Word of Wisdom:**

According to Kendall, it is the greatest gift and is the most accessible one. Simply it is the ability of having 20/20 foresight vision. It keeps us from making mistakes. It keeps us from making fools of ourselves. It is God's will for us to have this gift, but we need to ask Him. James 1:5 says that, "If any of you lacks wisdom, let him ask God, who gives to all liberally and without reproach, and it will be given to him." Kendall continues to say that sexual purity is one of the first qualifications for having wisdom. The first seven chapters in the book of "Proverbs" are given to warn us against adultery and sexual infidelity. He concludes that the fear of the Lord, especially in this area, is the source of all wisdom.

**Word of knowledge:**

---

[57] R.T. Kendall, *HolyFire* (Lake Mary, Florida: Charisma House,2014)pp 145-151.

It refers to special knowledge needed in crisis, in this case, it borders on the gift of wisdom. It may refer to supernatural knowledge for someone in a particular crisis. If so, it borders on the gift of prophecy.

## Faith

According to Kendall, it is not the faith of salvation;[58] otherwise it should not be listed as a gift of the Spirit to people already saved. It refers to a crisis situation. For someone in a particular crisis, it is easier to trust God to take to heaven than to get him through the day!

## Healing

Kendall talks about this gift from his own experience. He saw a lot of people healed when they prayed for the sick. In fact people who were healed were a few, not many. He recalls Oral Roberts, as he visited him at his home three times. Only during the years of 1952-1954,[59] had seen extraordinary healings, but not afterwards which means the gift of healing can come and go.

## Miraculous powers

Kendall asks, what is the difference between healings and miraculous powers? He explains that miracles are sudden, but healing is gradual. He recalls Act 3:16 when a forty-year-old man was instantly healed. Was it a miracle? Yes, surely. But it is a healing too. So, there is an overlap between miracles and healings like that between the word of knowledge and the gift of prophecy.

## Prophecy

---

[58] Later in the study, we will see it is the same "faith" of salvation, but grows to move mountains as in Mathew 17.

[59] The reader can go to "YouTube" and see some of these healings.

Paul urged the Corinthians to desire the spiritual gifts especially the gift of prophecy,[60] in the context of exhortation and encouragement of believers. Kendall warns against people saying "The Lord told me." Speaking like this is not only highly presumptuous, but is speaking the name of the Lord in vain.

### Distinguishing between spirits

This is a God-given ability to discern the true from the false, recognizing the Holy Spirit and also the demonic spirits. It is more important to discern the presence of the Holy Spirit than the demonic or satanic ones.

### Speaking in tongues

Kendall compares "speaking in tongues" mentioned in 1 Corinthians 14:2 and the "speaking in tongues" mentioned in Acts 2:4. In his opinion, they are not the same, as in the first verse, Paul relates the tongues to praying to God with other languages, which is not obvious in the latter verse. Kendall stresses, again, that if it were not the stigma of this particular gift, he does not think the gifts of the Spirit would be so controversial.

### Interpretation of tongues

It is the rarest of the gifts, but believers need to maintain integrity when exercising this gift. But if the interpretation is absolutely right, it can bring a great witness to God's glory (1 Cor.14:25).

Lastly, Kendall says, twice Paul says we should "eagerly desire" these gifts (1Cornith.12:31 and 1Cornith.14:1). The onus is on us all to show how closely we wish to adhere to the Scripture by coveting the gifts of the Holy Spirit. The question now is how the biblical counseling benefits from these awesome graces.

---

[60] 1 Corinthians 14:1

## The Biblical Counseling Movement

Glyn Harrison,[61] the Christian psychiatrist, says that biblical counseling attracts growing interest in the UK. In his article, titled, "The New Biblical Counseling" published in the "triple helix" (2011), he adopts the view of integrating the Christian faith with psychological methods. He says that the challenge the Christian psychiatrists and psychologists are facing today is to apply their faith in practice, as he sees the old certainties of counseling models continue to breakdown.

Harrison then explains that biblical counseling has grown out of the earlier work of Jay Adams. Adams coined the term "Nouthetic Counseling" in his influential book *Competent to Counsel,* first published in 1970. He attacked modern psychologists who replaced biblical categories of creation, fall, redemption and holiness with secular categories of health and illness. Adams founded the Christian Counseling Education Foundation CCEF, but he left the organization in the mid 1970s. The next generation of biblical counselors, like David Powlison, have followed his route. However the followers of Jay Adams have been more sensitive to suffering, whilst confronting the counselees of their sin.

Dr David Powlison(2010)[62] writes that in 1970, Jay Adams, a forty –one year old Presbyterian pastor and seminary professor, published an inflammatory book titled, "Competent to Counsel (CtC),"[63] which attacked the psychiatric establishment over the Church's thinking and practice. He was stimulated by the anti-psychiatrists of 0. Hobart Mower, William Glasser, Perry London, and Thomas Szasz. He initiated a

---

[61] Glynn Harrison article in "triple helix" Christian Medical Fellowship UK magazine, Easter edition, 2011, pp8-10, titled The New Biblical Counselling, a challenge to Christian' psychiatrists.

[62] David Powlison,*The Biblical Counselling Movement* (Greens boro,NJ: New Growth Press,2010)page XV11.

[63] The first book was written by Adams to introduce and explain his model, "Competent to Counsel, An Introduction to Nouthetic Counselling" First published in 1970.

revolutionized biblical counseling model known as Nouthetic[64] Counseling and wanted conservative Protestants to take care of their own and to stop referring people to psychiatric authorities. He also attacked the evangelical psychologists, even though they shared his conservative faith, because they integrated Christian faith with modern secular psychology.[65] In the 1980s, the evangelical psychologists, or so-called *the integrationists*, successfully asserted their claim to cultural authority over problems in living. They extended their power from churches to higher education institutions ignoring Adams' call, and continued to provide care for the Protestant conservatives. But again in the 1990s, biblical counseling started to prosper.

## Crabb's Model(Integration Model) versus Adams' Model (Biblical Model)

On one side, Larry Crabb,[66] the well-known integrationist, criticizes Adams' model by saying:[67]

1. The confrontational model of Adams does not cover all ingredients of effective Christian counseling. In Thessalonians 4:14, the Apostle Paul says that, "Now we exhort you, brethren,

---

[64] Adams model is based on confrontation of sin. It is the corner -stone of his model where the counsellor's main job is to confront the counselees of their sins to lead them to repentance and acceptance of God's forgiveness to solve their problems of living.

[65] They are known as Integrationists. Over the past 45 years or so, there has been a bitter conflict between them and the pure biblical counsellors led by Jay Adams.

[66] Larry Crabb is the well-known integrationist. He is the founder and director of the Institute of Biblical Community (formally the institute of Biblical Counseling), a ministry committed to training Christians to resolve life's problems biblically and to help others in the context of Christian community. He earned his Ph.D degree in clinical psychology from the University of Illinois in 1970. He published his first book, "Basic Principles of Biblical Counseling" in 1975, in response to Adams's book CtC . Other books like "Effective Biblical Counseling," where Colin Dye adopted his counseling manuals from.

[67] Larry Crabb, *Effective Biblical Counselling, A model for Helping Christians Becoming Capable Counsellors* (Grand Rapids, MI: Zondervan,1977) pp 147-151.

warn (confront and admonish) those who are unruly, comfort the fainthearted, uphold the weak, be patient with all." Crabb adds, to harshly confront a fainthearted person, not only would be cruel but also could be harmful.

2. Adams compares the behavior patterns (Crabb calls it goal-oriented behavior) with his understanding of biblical behavioral patterns and then commands change. Crabb asks, would a single key ingredient of God's command be sufficient to achieve change? He then disputes that by saying, it is the person's way of thinking (Crabb calls it assumption system) that should be changed and then only his/her behavior will be changed accordingly.

On the other side, Howard Eyrich(2002) [68] criticizes Crabb's model by saying, Crabbs' goal of counseling is to meet the person's needs. So he shifts the biblical model from God-centered to man-centered. The goal of biblical counseling should be rather healing of the counselee's wholeness (soul, mind and body) by bringing him/her to faith in Christ. Therefore, the counselor should seek first the conversion and consecration of the counselee. Only then can true joy and spiritual vitality be experienced.[69]

In this context also, John MacArthur writes under the title of "Failure of Christian Psychology."[70]

> The Church is ingesting heavy doses of dogma from psychology. Sin is called sickness, so people think it requires therapy instead of repentance. Habitual sin is

---

[68] Eyrich is Adams's disciple Appling the Nouthetic Counselling in his writing and counselling ministry. He structured a 10-stages counselling model that will be discussed later in Adams chapter.

[69] Eyrich, Howard and William Hins,*Curing the Heart, A Model for Biblical Counselling*(Rose Shire, UK: Monitor Publications,2002)page 162.

[70] John MacArthur,*Counselling, How to Counsel Biblically* (Nashville: Thomas Neslson,2005) pp14-15

called addiction or compulsive behavior, and many surmise its solution is medical care rather than moral correction. (MacArthur 2005, 14)

He then adds,

Human therapies are embraced, most eagerly by the spiritually weak, those who are shallow or ignorant of biblical truth. And who are unwilling to accept the path of suffering that leads to spiritual maturity and deeper communion with God. (MacArthur 2005, 15)

Perhaps one should refer to Jay Adams, who declares that biblical counselling in the biblical sense of the word; changing them, sanctifying them through the work of the Holy Spirit, as His Word is ministered to their hearts. The counselees need the regeneration work of the Holy Spirit and then, they can be counselled by putting off the works of the flesh and putting on the fruit of the Spirit. The Holy Spirit empowers them while they pursue His luscious fruit and that might be all they need from biblical counselling.[71]

---

[71] Jay Adams, Theology of Biblical Counselling, More than redemption (Grand Rapids, MI:Zondorvan,1979)page 251.

Chapter Three

# JAY ADAMS' MODEL OF BIBLICAL COUNSELING

Jay Adams has laid the foundation of his model, which is known as "Nouthetic Counseling." Its principles are outlined in his two books: "Complement to Counsel" (first published in 1970), followed by "The Christian Counselor's Manual" (first published in 1973). One of Adams's disciples, Dr Howard Eyrich (2002) [72]formulated Adams' principles into a structured model of 10 steps, to be adopted at the counseling sessions[73] (diagram 1).

Quite simply, Nouthetic Counseling is biblical counseling - it gets its name from the Greek word *noutheteo* which is usually translated "admonish" (Romans 15:14). It means "to confront as a friend" and was the normal method of counseling before modernists invented secular psychology in the early 1900s. According to Adams, Nouthetic Counseling is effective for believers and begins with the evangelism of those who are

---

[72] Howard Eyrich and William Hins' book, *Curing The Heart, A Model For Biblical Counselling* (Rose Shire,UK: Mentor Publications,2002).

[73] It has 10 steps: Building involvement, Gather Data,Isolate Problem, Determine Direction, Rethink Problem, Confrontation, Give Hope, Gain Commitment, Assign Homework, and Evaluate Homework. The counselor can start at any step and move forward or backward according to the progress of the case.

not believers because biblical counselors understand that only believers can understand the deep truths of God (1 Corinthians 2:14). The Holy Spirit is present in the counseling setting. God's Word change them (1 Corinthians 6:9-11; Galatians 5:16). Accordingly biblical or Nouthetic Counseling depends on the Holy Spirit to change the counselees. He enlightens God's Word as it is intended - to teach, rebuke, correct, and train in righteousness (2 Timothy 3:16).[74]

Powlison summarizes Adams's principles in biblical counseling by saying:

> Adams established goals for the church's counseling that employed the ingredients of the traditional Christian message. First, because man's greatest need is forgiveness, the forgiving grace of Jesus Christ was essential to solving problems in living. Adams believed that God worked within the human personality, and that those who were forgiven would also be helped by the Holy Spirit to alter patterns of thinking, feeling, and behavior. Second, as thankful recipients of such grace, "human beings should look like Jesus Christ." Thus Adams defined the change process, again in frankly theological terms, as "progressive sanctification."[75]

In the recent interview with Jay Adams in the Tabletalk magazine (2014),[76] Adams says that during his sixty-plus years of ministry, he has focused on two disciplines: Exegesis[77] and systemic theology. The

---

[74] www.GotQuestions.org,2002-2015,"What is nouthetic counselling?"

[75] David Powlison, *The Biblical Counselling Movement, History and Context,* (Greensboro, NC: Growth,2010)page 2

[76] Jay Adams, "Competent to Counsel: An Interview with Jay Adams," *Tabketalk Magazine.* 1ˢᵗ February 2014.

[77] Critical explanation or interpretation of a text. Oxford dictionary page 285.

combination of these two has kept him from going off-base when he began counseling and began to write about it. During all these years of counseling, he has been concerned to be biblically accurate and doctrinally correct from the start of his ministry.

Adams continues to say that, counseling is not a great thing – in itself - but becomes necessary whenever the rescue of a brother or sister is called for. The Scripture's view of counseling involves three Cs - Concern, Confrontation, and Change; our *concern* for a brother or sister in trouble spiritually; one lovingly *confronts* him in order to bring about *change* that is pleasing to God. Such change is brought about by the ministry of the Word in the power of the Holy Spirit, working both in the counselor and the counselee.

Additionally, in the interview, Adams expresses concern regarding the integrationists who are trying to combine the insights of psychology with those of the Bible. In providing such counseling, Scripture being bent to fit non-scriptural material that the counselor attempts to integrate with it. Adams believes that the task of integration is impossible without ending up in a non-scriptural method.

Diagram 1    The Ten-Step Model of Biblical Counseling[1]

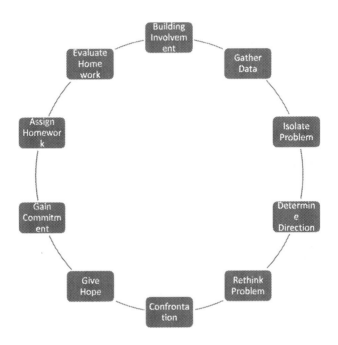

---
[1] Dr Howard Eyrich's book, "Curing the Heart" page 81.

# The Role of the Holy Spirit in Adams' Model of Biblical Counseling

Adams quotes what the Lord Jesus says in Mathew 18:20, "For where two or three are gathered together in My name, I am there to the midst of them." The verse closely follows the reconciliation passage in Mathew 18:15:17, and indeed it is part of it. So, Adams concludes that in the counseling room, at least, three persons should be present: The Lord Jesus' presence in the person of the Holy Spirit, the counselor and the counselee.[78] The Holy Spirit brings the reconciliation through His Word (The Scripture).

# Counseling and the Doctrine of Sanctification in Adams' model[79]

Adams (1979) stresses again that biblical counseling is for believers only, (with unbelievers, pre-counseling, -i.e., evangelism - is appropriate).[80] True counseling has to be done in depth; it is the work of the Spirit who makes the change from within. This takes place in the heart of a regenerate human-being, as he responds favorably to the ministry of the Word because of his new life tendencies in Christ. While regeneration (or justification) is an "Act" done entirely by God through the Holy Spirit,[81] progressive sanctification is a "Process," where God, through the Holy Spirit, *enables* man to live a holy and godly life.

---

[78] Jay E Adams, *The Christian Counselor's* (Grand Rapids, MI:Zondervan,1973)page 4.

[79] Jay E Adams, *A Theology of Christian Counselling, More Than Redemption* (Grand Rapids, MI: Zondervan, 1979) Pp233-248.

[80] The above text, in the appendix titled, "What to do when counsel an unbeliever." Pp 309-326.

[81] Regeneration is a broader term to include" conversion", which is also the work of the Holy Spirit. He gives man the wisdom and power to repent and believe in the Lord Jesus as the Saviour.

Adams explains further by saying that the goal of counseling is effective change. In his model, the required change is achieved by *putting off* the old ways of the pre-Christian life and *putting on* the new ones. General speaking, change is hard but in Christ there is a genuine basis for hope. [82]

Adams gives an example by saying, "When is a thief not a thief?" The answer when he stops stealing is not the right answer, because when he has no money to live, he has to steal to eat. By answering, when he labors and earns money, so he will stop stealing, is not the complete answer. The Apostle Paul says in Ephesians 4:22-24, "that you *put off*, concerning your former conduct. The old man which grows corrupt according to the deceitful lusts and *renew in the Spirit of your mind*; and that you *put on* the new man who was created according to God, in true righteousness and holiness." So, the complete answer is that the thief should put off stealing and put on working to earn money. This process of putting off and putting on is not complete unless he becomes a new man with a renewed mind in the Spirit.[83]

Another factor to consider is that bad behavior like swearing, lying, stealing, so forth, can become a habit, difficult to break, even after regeneration. We cannot assume that a thief or a liar wakes up suddenly one morning to see the change happening. He needs to de-habilitate from his old life style and re-habilitate to a different, new life style. The Holy Spirit here plays a major role. The Apostle Paul says in Ephesians 4:17, "walk no longer as the Gentiles walk." Verse 20-21, says, "But you have not so *learned* Christ, if indeed you have heard Him and have been taught by Him, as the truth is in Jesus." The change here also involves the change in life style, The renewal of mind and the change in the new life style,

---

[82] Jay E Adams, *A Theology of Christians Counselling* (Grand Rapids, MI: Zondervan, 1979) pp 234-236.

[83] This is to reply on Crabb's critics that Adams model of change works only at the behaviour level. Here, Adams says it is the whole person needs to be changed.

according to Adams, is a lifelong process to conform to Jesus' likeness. This process is called "Progressive Sanctification."[84]

The process of sanctification is the work of the Holy Spirit enabling man to live a life of godliness and holiness. But, how does the Holy Spirit work? The Holy Spirit Himself has plainly told us how He works. He ordinarily works *through* the Scripture. The Bible is the Holy Spirit's book. He inspired it. He always requires prayerful study and obedient practice of the Word of God. The counselor must insist on regular study of God's Word as an essential factor to achieve the change required.

## Counseling and the Spirit's Fruit in Adams' Model[85]

Adams (1973)[86] points out that part of the process of progressive sanctification[87] is to *put off* the works of the flesh[88] and to *put on* the fruit of the Spirit.

Adams goes on to talk about the "fruit" of the Spirit in Galatians 5:22-23. It is in the singular which means the believers should have it all. First, the fruit grows in those who have been given a new life through regeneration (entirely the Spirit's work). A sign of life is growth, producing fruit. Second, the Holy Spirit is the Person Who has planted it (by regeneration) and cultivated it (by sanctification, shared by man). Third, the role of man (the counselor to direct and the counselee to obey

---

[84] De-habilitation and rehabilitation process is explained in details in Adams' book, "A Theology of Christian Counselling."pp237-248.

[85] Jay E Adams, *A theology of Christian Counselling* (Grand Rapids, MI: Zondervan, 1979) pp. 249-262.

[86] Jay E Adams, *The Christian Counsellor Manual* (Grand Rapids, MI:Zondervan,1973) pp 344-347

[87] According to Adams, progressive sanctification involves also radical amputation of sinful temptations, suffering and perseverance.

[88] Sinful attitudes and actions as mentioned in Gallatin 5:19-21. The list is extensive to be examined, but it is self explanatory.

and commit) is to assist in producing it, but cannot initiate or assure its production. Fourth, the role of counselor is to minister the Word, work under the Spirit in His Orchard to provide such care. God, through His Spirit, enables the counselee to produce this fruit in his own life.

Adams continues by saying that, from the first glance at Galatians 5:22-23, one could see that the Apostle Paul precludes human effort. Is man passive, as in regeneration? Adams believes not. So, Adams looks at other texts in the Scripture to verify that. In 1 Tim. 6:11,the Apostle Paul says, "But you, O man of God, flee these things and *pursue* righteousness, godliness, faith, love, patience, gentleness." Also in 2 Tim. 2:22, "----*pursue* righteousness, faith, love, peace---." Adams notices that there is overlap between the items of the fruit of the Galatians 5 and those of Tim. 1 and 2. So, he concludes that the items of the fruit of the Spirit are not only 9 but 12 in total (by adding other three from Tim. one and two, which are not mentioned in the Galatians 5). Also there is human effort in the word *pursue.* [89] The Counselee is not just waiting for the fruit to come through the Spirit.

When Adams examines the fruit of the Spirit, produced in the life of a believer, he discovers that it can cause radical change in personality traits,[90] and the counselee who has learned to produce such luscious fruit in profusion, is a person who has overcome his difficulties and may need no further counseling.

---

[89] The pursue is an important human factor in the task of Christian counselling. According to Adams counselees sometimes all they do is to pray. Praying about a problem to be solved is important but it needs to be followed by action.

[90] Adams defines the personality trait as the basic nature with which one was born, how he has used and developed it in response to life, plus how God has changed and melded it up until the point of consideration.

## The Pursuit of Fruit in Counseling

Adams looks at *peace,* as an example, and how does a Christian pursue it? It is by applying the principle of putting off and putting on. In doing that, Adams quotes Philippians 4:6-9, as an example as follows:

1. *Putting off* (vss.6, 7): the heart and the mind cast cares on God in prayers. The prayers,general and specific, should be with thanksgiving both for the trial itself and in advance for what God will do about the problem
2. *Putting on* (verse 8): refilling the heart and mind with proper and productive thoughts and concerns
3. *Pursue* peace (verse 9) by doing what the Philippians had learned, heard and seen from the Apostle Paul who as a model, conformed to Jesus' likeness. So prayers should be followed by action.

## The Fruit That Is Our Pursuit

The twelve fruit of Galatians 5:22-23, 1Timothy 6:11 and 2Timathy 2:22, with a brief description of each, are as follows:

**1. Love:**

Love in Christian lives is the product of the Holy Spirit. No man unaided by the Spirit can attain it. It is the sort of love that God has for sinful men and women. Nothing is expected in return. Love should be the priority for Christians to pursue. Christians are required to love the unlovable.

**2. Joy:**

The Lord Jesus says in John 15:11,"These things I have spoken to you, that My Joy may remain in you, and that your joy may be full." John 16:24, He also says, "Until now you have asked nothing in My name. Ask and you will receive and your joy may be full." So, joy is closely associated with having a relationship with Christ through the person of the Holy Spirit. Ask God and He will answer, and then have joy. Joy comes with faith. A believer should have faith in the midst of his/her trials, believing that everything works together for good for those who love the Lord.[91]

### 3. Peace:

The Apostle Paul says in Romans 5:1, "Therefore, having been justified by faith, we have peace with God through our Lord Jesus Christ." In a positive way, peace may be considered as a joyous sense of well-being, knowing that one is right with God, as his/her sins have been forgiven.

### 4 and 5, Patience[92] and Endurance[93]:

In simple words, endurance is to learn to endure what one cannot change,[94] while patience is to put up with what one does not have to, for the sake of Christ and for the welfare of others.

### 6 and 7, Kindness, Goodness:

Kindness is the opposite of being severe and harsh as mentioned in Romans11:22, "Here we see how kind and how severe towards those who have fallen, but kind to you-if you continue in His kindness. But if you do not, you too will be broken off."GNB[95] Kindness is followed and accompanied by goodness in Galatians 5:22. Both are dealing with the relationship of one towards another. To understand the word goodness in the Bible, Adams refers to Romans 15:14, "Now I myself am confident concerning you my brethren, that you also are full of goodness, filled with

---

[91] Romans 8:28.

[92] NKJV: longsuffering.

[93] NKJV: patience in 1 Tim.5:11.

[94] R T Kendall, "The Thorn in the Flesh" (1999). He explains how to endure things in life like loneliness, disabilities, chronic illness etc.

[95] Good News Bible version

all knowledge, able also to admonish one another." In the last verse, *goodness* is a characteristic essential for good counseling. The word "admonish" describes one who does good towards others because he cares for them.[96]

## 8. Faithfulness[97]:

The concept here is straightforward, meaning reliability, trustworthiness and loyalty. Many scriptural passages denote that meaning but the most important is that we, as Christians, are stewards for all we have, to Christ who bought us by His precious blood when He died for us on the Cross.

## 9. Meekness[98]:

It is difficult to get the meaning right in the English language.[99] However, it does not mean weakness. There are two examples in the Bible for people of God whose this fruit was in full bloom; one in the OT and another in the NT. In the OT, Moses was meek in dealing with the stubborn Israelites. He led them in the wildness with gentleness and smoothness but also with firmness. In the NT, the example is the Apostle Paul. We saw this characteristic when he dealt with the Galatians with meekness as they wanted to go back to observe the Law of Moses, as a prerequisite of salvation.[100]

## 10. Self-control:

According to Adams, this characteristic carries a very important concept in counseling. The exercise of self control is a fundamental issue for many counselees. Felix lacked self control in Acts 24:25, "But as Paul went on discussing about goodness, *self-control* and the day of Judgment,

---

[96] Adams again highlights the meaning of neuthetic, which is to admonish or warn one another because he/she cares for him/her.

[97] The Greek word is *pistis* carries both meanings of faith and faithfulness.

[98] NKJV is mentioned as gentleness Gal. 5:23

[99] English equivalent is soft, gentle, Oxford English Dictionary, paperback page 524

[100] He also dealt with this serious matter in firmness.

Felix was afraid and said, 'You may leave now, I will call you again when I get the chance.'"[101] Counselors should advise counselees to restrain anger, sorrow, frustration, sexual desire, and so forth, and apply discipline in practice the proper biblical outlets for negative emotions.

## 11. Righteousness:

The Apostle Paul directs Timothy to "pursue" righteousness. Obviously it is not the righteousness of justification, but it is the desire of a believer to do all that is right in the eyes of God and men, according to the Word of God in the Scripture.

## 12. Godliness:

It is to think and behave in a godly way. It is to refer to God whilst thinking and doing deeds in daily living, business, study and so forth. It is opposite to the hypocrites whose their behavior does not reflect their evil thinking and attitude.

## Practical Application

Adams suggests that the counselors do a list of the fruit's items. With each item they record the following:[102]

1. The meaning
2. Some applications
3. Ways of promoting the item in the lives of the counselees
4. Key passages of the Scripture in which each one occurs.

---

[101] Good News Bible version

[102] Jay E. Adam, *A theology of Christian Counselling* (Grand Rapids, MI: Zondervan, 1979) page 262.

## Counseling and the Gifts of the Spirit in Adams' Model[103]

Adams tackles the gifts of the Spirit in a completely different way to tackling the fruit of the Spirit as outlined above. He points out that, unlike the fruit of the Spirit, in which the believers should have them all in cluster, the Spirit's gifts are distributed by the Spirit as Christ apportions them (Ephesians 4:7, NIV). In 1 Corinthians 12:11, the Apostle Paul says also, "But one and the same Spirit works all these things (the gifts), distributing to each one individually as He wills." So all Christians should have at least one gift and the Spirit provides them as He *wills*.

However, Adams extends the gifts to include, besides the ministry and activity gifts used at the church, other gifts. Although Adams does not give details about the nature of the latter gifts, it is concluded in the rest of his chapter that these gifts can be used in other areas of life, for example in leisure, work, community, and so forth. That is clear when he advises the counselors to help the counselees to discover their gifts to the extent that they might need to change or adjust their jobs to assist them in living life to their highest potential.

Regarding the charismatic gifts, the concern of this study, Adams explains the purpose of the gifts in general in 1 Corinthians 12:4-7, and then in 1 Corinthians 12:11, but he ignores the verses in between in 1Corinthians 12:8-10 which talk specifically about the charismatic gifts. These are: the word of wisdom, the word of knowledge, faith, healings, miracles, prophecy, speaking in tongues and interpretation of tongues. Perhaps he believes that these special gifts had ceased after the time of the apostles and the early church, as explained earlier.[104]

---

[103] Jay E Adams, *The Christian Counselor's Manual* (Grand Rapids, MI: Zondervan,1973) pp 343-347.

[104] In this context, Max Andres(1999),p62, explains the reason why some theologians believe that these charismatic gifts had ceased. They say, these gifts were given to the apostles and the early church to validate the message of the gospel, since the message is established; there is no need for such gifts now.

Adams outlines the following general biblical principles while discussing the Holy Spirit's gifts with the counselees:

1. Helping the counselees to stop trying to do what they do not have the gifts to do

2. Helping the counselees to discover, develop, and then live up to the potential that the measure of their gifts require

3. Helping the counselees to find the proper place for the exercise of their gifts

4. Helping the counselees to use their gifts for the good of the whole body, functioning in harmony with other Christians

5. Helping the counselees to accept their gifts and not to complain about the Spirit not dispensing different ones to them

6. Helping the counselees to appreciate the gifts that are given to others.

In conclusion, "Neuthetic" is the biblical counseling model that was rediscovered in 1970 by Jay Adams, when he first published his first book "Competent to Counsel." The secret of Adams' continuous success, in spite of numerous critics, is because he has had a solid biblical foundation based on exegesis and his sound theological background.

His model is based on confrontation of sin as a corner stone for change which is generally the goal of every counseling. The change is achieved by putting off the sinful behavior and putting on the godly biblical behavior. The Holy Spirit plays a major role in his model. The unbelievers should not be counseled unless they regenerate or convert, which is entirely the work of the Holy Spirit. The Holy Spirit then empowers the counselees to put off the works of the flesh and to put on fruit of the Spirit, the concern of this study, which is part of a life long process of "progressive sanctification." Progressive sanctification is the ultimate goal of Adams' model of biblical counseling. There is human effort in this process unlike the conversion. The counselors should encourage the counselees to pursue the Spirit's fruit recorded mainly in Galatians 5:22-23, which might be all the counselees' need from counseling.

Regarding the gifts of the Spirit, Adams widens the range of these gifts to include, besides the ministry gifts at church, other general gifts used in other areas of life. Adams ignores the specific charismatic gifts of 1Cornthains 1:11, the concern of this study. Perhaps he believes that these gifts had ceased because they were expressed in the early church to validate the message of the gospel. He believes that there is no need for such gifts now as the message of the gospel has already been established.

# Chapter Four

# THE FRUIT AND THE GIFTS OF THE HOLY SPIRIT WITH REFERENCE TO GOLDEN FEE

Although Gordon Fee has not developed or adopted biblical counseling models, unlike Jay Adams and Colin Dye respectively, he is included in this study for two main reasons. First, to enrich our understanding of the fruit and the charismatic gifts of the Holy Spirit. Second, the most important, his books reflect the main goal of the Holy Spirit which is to produce the real thing, the righteousness of God Himself in the person of Jesus Christ, so that His children reflect His likeness, which is indeed, the goal of biblical counseling.

## The Fruit of the Spirit

Fee (1996)[105] points out that when we received the Spirit at conversion, we have been invaded by the living God Himself, in the person of His Spirit whose goal is to infect us thoroughly with God's own likeness.

---

[105] Gordon D Fee, *Paul, the Spirit, and the People of God* (Grand Rapids, MI: BakerAcademic oublications,1996)Pp112-116."

Paul's[106] phrase for this infection is the fruit of the Spirit. The growing of this fruit is the long way on the journey of Christian conversion.

Fee looks at the list mentioned in Galatians 5:22-23. The list is a mirror image of Christ Himself, and thus also reflections of what spiritual people are. He comments on the singular word, "fruit." It is the product of the Spirit in one cluster with several kinds of items on it. As Adams mentioned in the previous chapter, it does not come automatically.[107] The Spirit produces the fruit as believers continually walk with the Spirit's help. It is misleading to refer to this list as the nine-fold fruit of the Spirit. The list is not intended to be exhaustive but representative. Paul concludes the list as "such things," meaning all other virtues similar to these. The list is not intended to regulate Christians' behavior by rules of conduct; rather it is the product of walking and living in the Spirit. Most of the items have to do with individual believers living in harmony with God in the Christian community, reflecting the image of Christ in the fallen world.

Fee (1994)[108] continues to say that Paul makes a contrast between the "works" of the flesh, and the "fruit" of the Spirit. This contrast is intentional and significant. "Works," on the one hand, puts emphasis on human endeavor. "Fruit," on the other hand, highlights divine empowerment. Bruce (2000)[109] explains further by saying that, the transition from the "old man" to the "new-man" after conversion reflects the change from the weakness of the "flesh" to the power of the "Spirit," brought about by Christ in the life of the new convert.

---

[106] The Apostle Paul, Fee continues to call him by his Christian name of "Paul." Paul was the greatest apostle of all, but he was a humble man like his master Jesus.

[107] Adams gathered 12 items of fruit as was explained earlier. But it needs human effort. It needs to be pursued.

[108] Gordon D Fee, *God's Empowering Presence* (Grand Rapids,MI: BakerAcademic Publications,1994) Pp 443-446.

[109] E E Bruce, *Paul, Apostle of the Heart Set Free* (Grand Rapids, MI: Eerdmans Publishing 2000) pp198-201.

Fee then makes a contrast between the fruit of the Spirit mentioned in Galatians 5, and the gifts of the Spirit mentioned in 1 Corinthians 12-14. According to him, they are both nine fold "such as" virtues. Both are representative, not exhaustive. Both are equally important and significant for the lives of the believers. Fruit is mentioned more than gifts in Paul's letters, that does not mean one is more important than the other. The fruit of the Spirit in Galatians 5, for example, fits well with the argument in the context of this Epistle.

A brief outline of the fruit as follows:

**Love:**

Fee explains why Paul puts "love" on the top of the list. Love captures the essence of the character of God as seen in His relationship with His people. Love expresses itself to the full in the self-sacrificial death of Christ on behalf of His enemies.

However, for Paul, this is not simply a theory or abstract reality. The Spirit has poured this love into his heart. Love is not to do or feel for another for the sake of one's own self- fulfillment, but rather a self-sacrificial giving of oneself for others.

**Joy:**

Life in Christ, or life in the Spirit, is the life of Joy. Joy characterizes the Christian community, the community that "rejoices in the Lord always." In contrast, the community which lives without Christ in the middle is the community that easily given to misery. In this context, the Apostle Paul says in Galatians 5:15: "But if you bite and devour one another, beware lest you be consumed by one another!"[110]

**Peace:**

---

[110] The Apostle Paul warns the conflict and relationship problems can destroy the people of God, producing misery not joy.

As with love and joy, peace is associated with God and His people. The God of peace has made Jew and Gentile one people, one body (Eph 2:14-17). He then urged them to "keep the unity of the Spirit through the bond of peace" (Eph.4:3).[111] In another context, Paul argues with the Colossians in 3:15, "And let the peace of God rule in your hearts, to which also you were called in one body: and be thankful." Peace, therefore, is primarily to do with the cessation of hostilities. Blessed are the peacemakers! The Spirit alone can produce such peace in our midst.

In this context, Prof. Everett Worthington (1999)[112] has developed an integrated model to solve marital conflict between couples. There is no mention of the Holy Spirit's fruit: peace, love, and joy, because his model is intended to be for Christian and non-Christian couples. As the result, although his model is very neat and sophisticated, it lacks the divine peace between couples which is only available through the Holy Spirit.

## Forbearance:[113]

Fee looks at the Greek origin of this which is *"makrothymia."* He says in some cases it carries the meaning of patience. But patience tends to be individualistic and in general is used for one to be patient in dealing with various life circumstances (e.g., burnt toast). But Paul means, in this context, forbearance towards others. It comes as companion to "kindness." Love in 1Corinthians, 13:4, is patient and kind (NKJV).

## Kindness:

Forbearance and kindness come together in 1Cornith. 13:4 verse as mentioned above. It describes God's character towards His people.

---

[111] Love, peace and joy are wonderful triad that solve most of the difficulties when people come for counselling.

[112] Everett L. Worthington, *Hope Focused Marriage Counselling,* (Dowers Grove, Illinois: InterVarsity Press,1999)Case study by Terry L Hight, counselling non-Christian couple, 269-284.

[113] NKJV longsuffering

Kindness expresses the active side of love, while forbearance expresses the passive side. In this context, God's grace is demonstrated in His kindness towards us.[114]

We can assume such fruit reflects the contrast to the works of the flesh, which the Spirit not only empowers us to endure the hostility or unkindness of others, but also, enables us to show kindness to them, actively pursuing their good. If longsuffering means not to "chew someone's head off," (Gal. 5:15), kindness means to find ways to bind up his/her wounds.

## Goodness:

The adjective "good" describes God's character, God is good. Similarly, believers are described as full of goodness. Romans 15:14 says, "Now, I myself am confident concerning you, my brethren, that you also are full of goodness, filled with all knowledge, also able to admonish one another."[115]

Fee concludes that for Paul, he sums up by saying, in Galatians 6:9-10, "let us do good to all people." Those who sow in the Spirit are those who do good to all.

## Faith(fullness):

The Greek word here *"pistis"*[116] *means* God's faithfulness towards His people as in Romans 3:3. That unfaithfulness of God's people does not call into question God's own faithfulness. However, according to Fee, it is difficult to generalize the word to include one's faithfulness in relationship to others, as there is no text in the NT with such usage. But in the context

---

[114] Ephesians 2:7.

[115] Admonish means "warns seriously" (Oxford Dictionary page 10). Adams model of confrontation or Nouthetic counselling is based on this context. But admonishing with love, goodness is what Paul means here.

[116] As mentioned before, "pistis" carries the meaning of both faith and faithfulness. Here Fee says that the context refers to faith as trusting God, also God's faithfulness towards His people. Faithfulness of people towards each other is not the meaning in Galatians 5:22, according to Fee.

of Galatians 5, we can assume that faithful devotion to God will express itself towards others by means of other fruit in the list. True faith in God in this sense, as an item of the Spirit's fruit, expresses itself in love. Galatians 5:6, says "For in Christ Jesus, neither circumcisions nor un-circumcisions avails anything, but faith working through love."

**Gentleness:** [117]

As mentioned earlier, when discussing the fruit of the Spirit with Adams, Moses' character would be the best example to exhibit gentleness as seen when he dealt with the Israelites in the OT. But here Paul is a good example himself, when he dealt with the Galatians. In that context, he reflects the character of Christ.

It is difficult to translate the word in the English language.[118] However the word carries the sense of humility towards oneself. It is this fruit that Paul appeals to in Galatians 6:1, when he argues that those who walk in the Spirit can restore a brother or sister overtaken in fault. We need also, as counselors, to do the same, in the "Spirit of gentleness." Not only because the life of another person is at stake, but also, because we thereby remember our own fragilities and susceptibility to temptation.

**Self-Control:**

This word on this list is unique: first, it does not appear in the Scripture in any way as a character of God. Second, it appears in 1 Corinthians 7:9 with reference to sexual continence, and in 1 Corinthians 9:25 with regard to self-discipline of the athletes. Third, it is only aimed at the individual believer.

Self control stands against the first three works of the flesh (adultery, fornication, uncleanness) and/or excessive drunkenness and revelries.

---

[117] Translated in NKJV as "meekness"

[118] Adams also mentioned this difficulty.

Fee concludes that the Spirit's presence is the crucial matter, but His presence does not automatically ensure a quickened, fervent Spiritual life. The individual needs to keep the Spirit aflame. It is achieved by mutual encouragement and growth.[119]

## The Charismatic Gifts of the Holy Spirit (The Spirit and Charismata)

As mentioned before, Fee (1996)[120] classifies the gifts of the Holy Spirit into three groups hinted at in 1 Corinthian 12:4-6: service, miracles, and inspired utterances. The service gifts are those used in the ministry of the church like giving, caring, helpful deeds, guidance, and so forth, suggested for example in Romans 12:7-8. Fee says that these latter gifts are the Spirit's activities within the church and to include these as charismatic makes the category useless. The other two groups can be regarded as charismatic gifts.[121]

Fee (1994)[122] mentions another popular grouping of the charismatic gifts of 1 Corinthians 12:1-11, recorded by Baird (1994) which is (1) gifts of instruction (wisdom and knowledge); (2)gifts of supernatural power (faith, healings, miracles); and (3)gifts of inspired utterance (prophecy, discerning S/spirits, tongues, interpretation of tongues).[123]

Fee continues to say that what distinguishes this listing is the concretely visible nature of these items, especially of the last seven. These are, after

---

[119] Adams stresses on "to pursue," an active human effort to get the Spirit's fruit.

[120] Gordon D Fee, *Paul, the Spirit and the People of God* (Grand Rapids,MI: BakerAcadmic Publication,1996)163-178

[121] Oxford dictionary: charismatic gifts in the Christian faith are special gifts given by God, p138.

[122] Gordon D Fee, *God Empowering Presence,*(Grand Rapids, MI: BakerAcademic Publication,1994164-173.

[123] E.g., W. Baird, *The Corinthian Church-A Biblical Approach to Urban Culture,*(New York: Abingdon, 1994)139

all, not only "gifts," they are above all *manifestations* of the Spirit's presence in the midst. They are, like tongues,[124] extraordinary and supernatural phenomena.[125]

### The message of wisdom

Fee explains why Paul uses the word "message."[126] It means either (1) "a message/utterance of full wisdom," or (2) "an utterance characterized by wisdom." Both meanings are correct. Fee explains the first meaning by saying that the message of wisdom in the context of 1 Corinthians 2:10-13, is the full wisdom for man to understand the mind of God, regarding Christ's crucifixion to redeem His fallen creature. It is the highest wisdom revealed to man.

For the second meaning, Kendall (2014)[127] explains the "utterance characterized by wisdom" by saying, not everyone who was converted and filled with the Holy Spirit has such gift of wisdom. People might have natural wisdom before they were converted. It is there in their genes. However, according to James 1:5, it is mandatory for every Christians to ask for the gift of wisdom. When given, it is for a particular situation. In counseling, for example, a counselor should ask for the Spirit of wisdom to help a counselee in solving out a specific problem. So this gift is not a universal wisdom.

### The message of knowledge

Some argue that this gift is related to receiving Christian insight into the meaning of the Scripture, but if this is the case, it should not be classified as a supernatural gift. It is because of the word "message/

---

[124] Calls by Fee, the problem child and his companion: tongues and interpretation, 165.

[125] They are beyond the believer's natural abilities and training.

[126] NKJV: the word of wisdom.

[127] R.T. Kendall, *In Pursuit of His wisdom* (London, UK: Hodder and Stoughton,1999)95-97.

utterance," makes the wisdom or knowledge charismatic.[128] However, Fee notices it lies between "revelation" and "prophecy," (1 Corinthian 14:16), so it is most likely relating to, or bordering on revelation.[129] To support this claim, knowledge will cease, along with tongues and prophecy in heaven after the rupture of the church (1 Corinthians 13:8).

## Faith

With this word Paul moves on to include several more clearly supernatural manifestations of the Spirit. Faith here is the supernatural conviction that God will reveal his power or mercy in a special way in a specific instance. It is faith that moves the mountains. However according to Fee it is the same faith of salvation, contrary to what Kendall mentioned earlier in this study.[130] Also, as explained earlier, the Greek word "pistis" carries the meaning of both faith and faithfulness. In Galatians 5:22, "faith" (=faithfulness) is listed as a "fruit" of the Spirit.

## Gifts of healings

These are supernatural healings.[131] What is of interest here, according to Fee, is the language "gifts of healings," which recurs in the two lists in vv.28 and 30. Probably this language reflects two things: (a) the "manifestations" is given not to the person who is healed,[132] but to the person God uses for the healing of another; (2) the plural suggests not a permanent "gift," as it was with the Lord Jesus, but that each occurrence is a "gift" in its own right.

---

[128] J.D.G Dunn, *Jesus, Paul and the Law,* (Philadelphia: Westminster, 1999) 221.

[129] Revelation of something, that is impossible to know by natural abilities or senses.

[130] According to 2 Corinthians 4:13

[131] The messianic age, God would heal His people from their sickness: Mathew's use in 8:17 also Isaiah 53:4.

[132] The healings of non-believers can occur by a believer used as an instrument by the Holy Spirit.

**Workings of miracles:**

These cover all other kinds of supernatural activities beyond the healing of the sick. It is in pleural as healings, signifying also it is not a permanent manifestation in the believers.[133] Miracles were also a common manifestation of other Pauline churches, as evidenced in Galatians 3:4.

**Prophecy:**

Of all the charismata, this is the one mentioned most often in Paul's letters (Example: 1 Thessalonians 5:20, I Corinthians 11:4-5, Romans 12:6, and Ephesians 2:20). It is an orally delivered message at the gathered assembly, for the edification or encouragement of people. However all prophesying must be "discerned" by the Spirit-filled community. The goal is to strengthen the people of God so that they come to maturity in Christ (Ephesians 4:12).

According to Fee (1994), prophecy is often the word spoken of regarding a future event, but that is only one element, not necessary the crucial one. Further, in chapter 14 of 1 Corinthians, it consists of a spontaneous,[134] Spirit-inspired, intelligible message, orally delivered in the gathered assembly, intended for the edification or encouragement of the people. The implication also in chapter 14, is that this gift is widely available for all. The prophetic message should be "weighed" or "tested" never to be raised to the level of "inspired text." It should not be for a private personal matter, but if so, it needs affirmation by the elders of the church. So prophecy here is a community affair.

Fee, in another book (1996),[135] says that prophecy is connected to "revelation" in 1 Corinthians 14:6. According to him, it is difficult to conclude, whether prophecy means "revealing mysteries," or is straightforward for edification, comfort, and exhortation. He quotes 1

---

[133] The Holy Spirit manifestation of miracles when there is a necessity of doing them.

[134] In the sense that it is not a prepared sermon.

[135] Gordon Fee book Paul, the Spirit and the People of God, 170-172

Thessalonians 4:19-22 when Paul exhorts: "Do not quench the Spirit; do not despise prophesying; but test all things, and hold fast to the good and abstain from every evil expression."

### Discernment of S/spirits

Fee (1996)[136] includes this charismatic gift among the group of inspired utterances. The "Spirit" with capital letter "S," I presume, relates to the Holy Spirit. The "spirits" with a small letter "s," I presume, refers to evil spirits other than the Holy One who is the Spirit of God. So the spirits are in pleural in 1 Corinthians 12:10, "discerning spirits." Referring to Kendall earlier, it is more important to discern the Spirit of God in the assembly than discerning the evil spirits.

However, Fee, in another book (1994),[137] explains this gift by saying that it carries a considerable debate and little agreement among scholars. 1 John: 4-1, the Scripture says, "Beloved, do not believe every spirit, but test the spirits, whether they are of God; because many false prophets have gone out into the world." So, it is clear here that this gift relates to the ability to discern what is truly of the Spirit of God and what comes from other spirits.

But there are reasons to say that this gift is meant to help to discern prophecies. (a) 1 Corinthians 14:29, Paul calls for "discerning" or "testing" prophetic utterance. (b) 1 Corinthians 12:10, this gift immediately follows "prophecy," and is followed by "tongues," and interpretation of tongues, so it deals with discerning these utterances. The real difficulty lies with the word "spirits." Fee concludes that discerning "spirits" refer to differentiating the prophetic utterances by the others in the community who also have the Spirit and so can discern what is truly of the Holy Spirit.

---

[136] Fee; "Paul, the Spirit, and the People of God," 168.

[137] Fee; "God's Empowering Presence," 169-172.

## Speaking in Tongues:[138]

Fee suspects that " speaking in tongues and the interpretation of tongues" brought about all the arguments[139] in the assembly, and Paul uses prophecy as representative of all intelligible inspired utterances that are to be preferred to tongues in that setting.

As with prophecy, enough is said in 1 Corinthians: 12-14 to give us a fair idea as to how Paul understood it. The following seems certain:

1. Speaking in tongues is a "Spirit inspired utterance" (1 Corinthians 12:7, 11 and 14). So for people, who try to eliminate them altogether, should be careful as that could be regarded as an offense to the Holy Spirit.

2. The speaker is not ecstatic or out of control. Quite the opposite, the speaker in church should be silent when there is no interpreter. They should speak in turn if there is more than one. So the mind is not detached but at rest and "unfruitful" (1 Corinthians 14:27-28).

3. The speech is unintelligible, both to the speaker and the hearer, that is why it must be interpreted in the assembly (1Cornthians 14-14).

4. The speech is towards God (1 Corinthians 14:2, 14-15,28), so it should not be directed towards others.

5. As a gift in private prayer, Paul held it in the highest regard as seen in 1 Corinthians 12.

What is not certain is whether Paul understood it to be an actual earthy language is not clear, but the overall evidence suggests not.[140]

## The interpretation of tongues

---

[138] Fee; " Paul, the Spirit and the People of God," 168-170, also "GEP," 172-173.

[139] Similar to Kendall in this respect, if the gifts of tongues are not there, there would be no arguments about the charismatic gifts in general.

[140] Contrary to what John Sherrill says in his book, "They Speak with other tongues." (2004)

This is the obvious companion to "tongues," because of the intelligibility of the latter. It is to put into words what the tongues- speaker has said. It is too a" Spirit-inspired" gift of utterance and it is given either to the tongues-speaker or to another in the assembly (Corinthians 14:5, 13 and 27-28).

Finally, Fee comments on the views of those scholars who claim that these charismatic gifts as recorded in 1 Corinthians 12:1-11 (the concern of this study) are ceased by saying:

> Perhaps the greatest tragedy for the church is that it lost touch with the Spirit of God in its ongoing life, and as a result it often settled for what ordinary. Equally grievous is the urgency of some to justify such shortsightedness. The hope of course, lies with verse 11, that the one and the same Spirit will do as He pleases, despite the boxes provided for Him by those on both sides of this issue.[141]

The question now is how we make use of these charismatic gifts of the Holy Spirit in counseling? There is a lot to say about the Spirit's wisdom, faith, healings, and so forth in the counseling sessions. That is exactly what I will do in the last chapter.[142]

---

[141] Gordon D Fee, *God's Empowering Presence* (Grand Rapids, MI: BakerAcademic, 1994),175.

[142] Fee is very sure that the charismatic gifts will continue as long as we are waiting for the final consummation, the second coming of our Lord Jesus Christ.

## Chapter Five

# COLIN DYE'S ADOPTED MODEL OF BIBLICAL COUNSELING

Colin Dye (2012)[143] introduced his model of biblical counseling to lay the foundation for a Christian counseling ministry in the church. He originally planned to write three counseling manuals, roughly corresponding to the three counseling levels suggested by Larry Crabb around 35 years ago in his book, *Effective Biblical Counseling* (1977).[144]

The three counseling levels are:

Level I, Problem Feelings- ENCOURAGEMENT- Biblical Feelings[145] (Manual 1).
Goal: emotional change.
Level II, Problem Behavior- EXHORTATION- Biblical Behavior[146] (Manual 2).
Goal: emotional and behavioral change.

---

[143] Colin Dye, *Shaped by Grace, An Introduction to Biblical Counselling* (London UK: KT publication,2012)5-6

[144] Larry Crabb, *Effective Biblical Counselling,* (Grand Rapids, MI: Zondervan,1977).

[145] Colin Dye's first book of the series, "Shaped by Grace."(2012)

[146] Colin Dye's second book of the series, "Loving Obedience." (2013)

Level III, Problem Thinking- ENLIGHTENMENT- Biblical Thinking[147]
(Manual 3).
Goal: emotional, behavioral and cognitive change.

In his first manual[148], he defines secular counseling, where God is excluded in the process of counseling. In contrast, Christian counseling[149] is based on the biblical revelation that God is the ultimate reality. He is the originator and creator of all things. Without Him, we cannot discover the true meaning and purpose of life. Acts 17:28 says, "For in Him, we live, and move and have our being."

Biblical counseling[150], according to Dye, is based on the biblical doctrine that human beings are lost through sin. Sin has resulted in a broken relationship with God. However, through the redemption that God provided in Christ, our relationship with God is restored.

In salvation, we repent our sins and accept the forgiveness that is offered by grace, when Christ died for our sins on the Cross. Christ rose from the dead on the third day. He is glorified, and now He intercedes for us, according to Hebrews 7:25. The salvation ultimately leads to healing and restoration of the entire human personality - spirit, mind and body. Salvation includes our past (Justification) and our present (Sanctification) as well as our future (Glorification).

---

[147] This manual has not been published yet as planned, would it be published in the future, no one knows.

[148] First manual Pages 11-14

[149] The language here is important, Christian counselling acknowledges God in the process. It includes good counselling. (Harrison, CMF journal "triple halix "2011 Easter edition, 08), as well as biblical counselling.

[150] The basic principles of biblical counseling are: salvation, followed by sanctification, while dealing with the problems.

Christian counseling[151] is a mean of sanctification, where the goal of counselors is to help the counselees in this process. In other words, the counselors help the counselees in their journey to become more like Christ. *This is only possible through the enabling power and the transforming presence of the Holy Spirit.* [152]

David Benner (2002) explains further what is meant for a believer to become like Christ. He says after salvation, the Holy Spirit empowers him/her to live in a lifelong process of sanctification. Acquiring the fruit of the Spirit is part of this process.[153]

However, unlike Adams, Dye does not object to counseling non-Christians. He suggests that the approach will be different to help them to find solutions appropriate to where they are in life, with the ultimate aim of leading them to Christ.[154]

Another aspect, which differs from Jay Adams, is that biblical counseling can be integrated with secular psychology. Dye says, in this case, the psychological theories should be examined in the light of biblical revelation and only those elements that are consistent with Scripture are included.[155] But how does he apply the fruit and the charismatic gifts of the Holy Spirit in his integration model of counseling, which is the concern of this study?

In this context, it is worth looking at what Dye (2007) writes about this issue:

---

[151] This is Colin Dye's wording but not all Christian counsellors acknowledge that, only those who follow the footsteps of Jay Adams, as explained earlier.

[152] The above principles are agreed by Jay Adams as outlined in chapter 3.

[153] D.G Benner, *Sacred Companions: The Gifts of Spiritual Friendship and Direction* (Downers Grove:Intervarsity Press, 2002)31-39.

[154] Dye's first manual "Shaped by Grace." Page17

[155] The same reference above, under subheading, "Psychology and the Bible "pp 21-22

All change that is not motivated by and performed in the power of the Holy Spirit is sub-Christian and fundamentally unpleasing to God.

The aim of Christian counseling is to see the counselee free from bondages, sinful practices and erroneous thinking, so that he or she grows in *the fruit and gifts* of the Holy Spirit.[156]

---

[156] Colin Dye, *Ministry in the Spirit* (London, UK: KT publications,2007)15.

60

Diagram 2:    **Crabb's "Seven-Stages" Model of Change** [1]

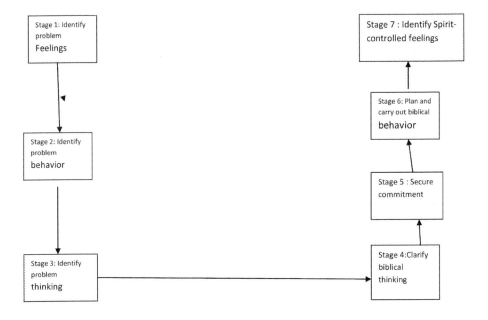

[1] Crabb's book, "Effective Biblical Counselling" page 160

## Dr Larry Crabb's Model of Biblical counseling (the Integration Model)

Although Larry Crabb is not included in the study, his integration model is adopted by Colin Dye. So it is worth looking at Crabb's model of counseling, before commenting on the benefits of the fruit and the charismatic gifts of the Holy Spirit in Dye's manuals, which is the focus of this study. Here, the core strategy of Crabb's counseling process is examined. Such things as how to keep the conversation running on profitable lines, how to handle specific counseling crisis like suicide and what to do with a very resistant client, [157] are skipped.[158]

Crabb's (1977) model consists of 7 stages,[159] as outlined in diagram 2. To explain how a Christian counselor manages problem cases by applying Crabb's integration model, the following real life case scenario is studied. It is about a woman with a problem of compulsive fornication.

In his book, "Counseling. How to Counsel Biblically," John MacArthur writes:

> I heard a popular Christian broadcast that offers live counseling to callers nationwide. A woman called and said, she had had a problem with compulsive fornication for years. She said she went to bed with "anyone and everyone" and felt powerless to change her behavior. The counselor suggested that her conduct was her way of striking back, a result of wounds inflicted by her passive father and overbearing mother. "There is no simple road to recovery," this radio therapist told her. "Your problem won't go away immediately" – it is an addiction, and

---

[157] In the Crabb's model, he calls the counselee client.

[158] There are other books of Crabb dealing with these issues, like "Inside Out." (1998)

[159] Larry Crabb. *Effective Biblical Counseling*,(Grand Rapids, MI:Zondervan,1977) 146-160.

those things require extended counseling. "You will need years of therapy to overcome your need for illicit sex." The suggestion was then made to the caller to find a supportive church that would be tolerant while worked her way out of "the painful wounds" that were "making her fornication." [160]

So the Christian counselor[161] manages this case as follow:

1. Stage 1: Identify problem feelings, where the counselor asks first, how a client feels about the problem. According to Crabb, there are 5 main problem emotions: anxiety, resentment, guilt, despair, and a vague sense of emptiness. For this woman, she has resentment towards her parents (or the counselor convinces her to have such feeling), but also she feels the sense of guilt because of her behavior, given the Christian background. Once the counselor identifies the problem feelings, he/she moves to the next stage.

2. Stage 2: Identify goal-oriented (problem) behavior. In this case, resentment towards her parents leads to her compulsive fornication, according to the opinion of the counselor.

3. Stage 3: Identify problem thinking. A faulty assumption leads to problem emotion and problem behavior. According to Crabb, human beings strive for two main purposes in life: to be significant and secure. In this context, Kenneth Pargament (2007)[162]describes what he calls " Sacred Domain," that a human being's main psychological need is to be safe and secure; also to be valued. Things like religion, material things like money, job, or even sex

---

[160] John MacArthur, *Counselling, How to Counsel Biblically* (Nashville: Thomas Nelson, 2005)15.

[161] The Christian counsellor who applies the integration model similar to Crabb's one.

[162] Kenneth I Pargament, *Spirituality Integrated Psychotherapy* (New York, NY: The Guilford Press, 2007)29-52.

or alcohol are regarded as either good or bad sacred domains. A person holds firmly to his/her sacred domain because losing it disturbs his/ her peace of mind and internal security. The role of a counselor (whether secular or Christian) is to identify the bad sacred domain, and tries to transfer the bad one to a good one or to remove the bad one completely from the client's mind.

The same principle here is applied in Crabb's model, but instead of good and bad sacred domains, he names them as good and wrong assumptions. In this case, the bad sacred domain or wrong assumption is compulsive sex. According to Crabb, in biblical counseling, saying to the counselee that the Lord Jesus provides her with the security and value she needs, is not enough. So once the unbiblical assumption[163] is identified, the hard work begins to change this faulty assumption. In doing that the counselor needs to follow the following steps:

A. *Identify where the wrong assumption was learned*: when the client sees that outer circumstances were responsible for teaching her this fornicating behavior, she will realize that her assumption can be faulty. Here, she was told that the problem was related to her father who was passive and her mother who was overbearing. The correction of her behavior is easier then, when she realizes that.[164]

B. *Encourage expression of emotions surrounding the belief*: In this case, she feels resentment towards her father, but at the same time, guilt towards herself because of her indecent behavior, as explained earlier. As the result of

---

[163] Wrong assumption/ bad sacred domain are called unbiblical while the good ones are called biblical according to Crabb.

[164] This is the problem of the secular psychologists in general. Sometimes, or might be always, they make assumptions that do not make sense!

this explanation, the client feels understood, she will relax and be less defensive in considering the validity of her thinking.

C. *Support the client as she considers changing her assumption*: Crabb says, to give up a long-held assumption is difficult, especially if that threatens her security and significance (or her sacred domain as explained above). So the client needs an *encouraging* environment in this process, which is to find out a *tolerant* church to support her. Crabb says, "Some therapists speak of ego borrowing." He then quotes 1 Thessalonians 5:14, where the Apostle Paul's advice is to uphold the weak.[165]

D. *Teach the client what to fill her mind with*: the "Tape Recorder" Technique[166]: Crabb suggests that the client should write about 35 cards with her wrong assumptions and contrast these with the same number of biblical commands, and keep these cards in her pocket. Every time she has a wrong assumption, she reads the biblical alternative instead. In this way, she will enforce the biblical assumptions.

4. Stage 4: Clarify Biblical Thinking as outlined above.

5. Stage 5: Secure Commitment:[167] according to Crabb, confession of sin seems most appropriate at this stage. With confession, she should commit to not sinning again. Now she is armed with

---

[165] This is the culprit of the inegrationists, they call sin illness or weakness, and the sinners need support and encouragement.

[166] This technique is quite similar to the well-known secular model of "Stages of Change": pre-contemplation, contemplation, preparation, action, and maintenance without confrontation. (Connors et al, 2001)

[167] Stage 5 is a new stage not mentioned in Crabb's earlier book (1975), "Basic Principles of Biblical Counselling."

*"her new thinking that significance and security do not depend on her fornication, but on God."* Crabb quotes Mathews 6:33 which teaches that God will supply our material needs if we seek first His righteousness.

6.  Stage 6: Plan and Carry out Biblical Behavior: in this case, the client should put an end to her adulterous life to live in purity.

7.  Stage 7: Identify Spirit-Controlled Feelings: Crabb comments upon the wonderful sense of improved adjustment with spiritual peace and quietness which follow a renewed mind (stage4), commitment (stage 5), and obedience (stage 6).

MacArthur comments on the management of the above case by saying: What kind of advice is that? First, the counselor gave the woman permission to disobey a clear command of Scripture: "flee immorality" (1 Cor. 6:18). Second, he blames her parents and justifies her resentment toward them. Third, he thinks she could decrease gradually from her sin, under therapy, of course. Worse of all, he encourages churches to tolerate a person with sexual sin, until therapy begins to work, in a national radio broadcast! MacArthur concludes by saying, there is no biblical justification for such counsel; in fact, it goes against God's Word. The Apostle Paul told the Corinthian church to turn the adulterer over to Satan, putting him out of the church (1 Corinthians 5).

However, there is a simple solution to this woman's problem. It is God's empowering presence, the Person of the Holy Spirit. Galatians 5:16 says, "Walk by the Spirit and you will not carry out the desire of the flesh."

So, is there a role of the Holy Spirit in Crabb's integration model? The answer is not. The Holy Spirit is ignored in his model. Here is some evidence of that:

1.  The word "parakaleo" is a Greek word which was used originally by the Lord Jesus to refer to the Holy Spirit, when He says in John 15:16, " And I will pray the Father and He will give you another

*Helpe*r (parakaleo), that He may abide with you forever." Crabb uses this word "parakaleo" to describe the human counselor who should comfort, encourage and help the counselee, ignoring the Holy Spirit role in this respect.[168]

2.  In stage 4 of Crabb's model, when he explains that the client needs support from the church while he/she is going through the process of change, Crabb uses the term "ego borrowing" which means the client borrows strength from "the ego" of the counselor or church members, ignoring God's empowering strength available in the Holy Spirit who dwells in the believers. [169] Anyway the Holy Spirit does not support things against His holiness; the client should repent these sinful deeds. The counselor and the church should do the same.

3.  In stage 7, Identify Spirit- Controlled Feelings, Crabb uses the vague word "Spirit,"[170] that leaves the reader wondering, who is the Spirit that Crabb refers to? Is that the Holy Spirit or other pagan spirits? For example, the Buddhists offer inner peace through the meditation which is part of worship in their religion.[171] In this context also, Mohamed Salem and John Foskett (2010) diverge spirituality to include other religions like Islam and Hinduism. [172] In this context, Jeremiah 17:9, warns us against these rituals by saying, "The Heart is deceitful above all things, and desperately

---

[168] Larry Crabb, *Effective Biblical Counselling*(Grand Rapids MI:Zondervan,1977),148.

[169] Same reference above page 155.Although that can be true, but the emphasis of the church or the church members is to encourage the person in trouble to use first his/her resources in the Spirit .The Holy Spirit does not support adulterous sin as in the above case. So perhaps Crabb is trying to avoid the Holy Spirit in this aspect.

[170] The same reference above page 159.

[171] For reference visit website www.thekchencentre.org

[172] Chris Cook, Andrew Powell, and Andrew Sims, ed, *Spirituality and Psychiatry*, Chapter 12, *Religion and religious experiences* by Mohamed Salem and John Foskett (London, UK: RCPsych .publications, 2010)233-253.

wicked; who can know it? That is why one of the gifts of the Holy Spirit is "discerning the S/spirits"[173] (1 Corinthians 12:10).

## The Fruit and the Gifts of the Holy Spirit in Colin Dye's Counseling Manuals

### Level I Counseling, Manual One [174]

Dye (2012)[175] explains level I. It revolves around encouragement; a Christian believer, who is not professional, encourages another believer to change his/her problem feelings from a negative emotion to a biblical or positive one. For example from being sad and overwhelmed with problems of life to a joyful, thankful to God because he knows that God is good and in control, and all things work together for those who love the Lord.[176] No formal training is required for this level of counseling.

Dye(2012) says that every member of the church should do this task of encouraging other members who go through difficulties. Because no training is required for this level of counseling, every church member should be prepared to do this role.

Dye explains key themes of encouragement. In level 1 counseling manual, he does not integrate psychological ideas or terms like "ego borrowing," like Crabb does, but he examines a passage in the Scripture to explain how a believer in the church, without previous training in psychology, becomes a good encourager of others.

---

[173] Skilfully, Gordon Fee when he explains this Holy Spirit gifts, he writes "S/spirit "; "S" in a capital letter refers to the Holy Spirit, the Spirit of God. The others are beginning with a small letter "s" and the word is in pleural referring to other pagan spirits: Fee's book, "Paul, the Spirit and the People of God." page 168.

[174] According to Crabb's model that Dye adopted, level I counselling is not about solving a problem or bringing correction. Usually it is directed toward giving quick, grip responses to a problem perceived by the counsellor.

[175] Colin Dye's book, "Shaped by Grace" pp 69-76.

[176] Romans 8:27

First, he defines the word "encouragement." It is the act of supporting and helping others. It has two basic elements. First: by what you say or do you give someone confidence, support or hope. Second: by what you say or do you cause and encourage a given response. This level is not dealing with correction, which is the goal of level II counseling, according to Dye.

Dye then explains key themes of encouragement. He quotes John 15:1-17 for this purpose. These themes are studied here because it is related to the topic of this study, which is the benefits of the fruit and the charismatic gifts of the Holy Spirit in biblical counseling. In this passage, the Lord Jesus talks about the Holy Spirit and there is an overlap of the items of the fruit of the Spirit mentioned in this passage with the ones of Galatians 5:22-23, specifically love and joy.

1. John 15:3 says, "You are clean because of the Word which I have spoken to you." The counselee is assured of God's unconditional acceptance. Because of the Grace, the counselee is unconditionally loved, totally forgiven and eternally accepted in Christ.

2. John 15:5 says, "I am the vine; you are the branches." Here the counselor explains to the counselee that the life of Christ, in the person of the Holy Spirit,[177] is in the counselee and in brothers and sisters of the church.

3. John 15:5 says, "I am the vine; you are the branches." The church is the family of God; the members are connected to each other by Christ. They are here to help, lift up and strengthen one another.

4. John 15:16 says, "You did not choose me, but I chose you and appointed you that you should go and bear fruit, and that your fruit should remain, that whatever you ask the Father in My name He may give you." The counselee has the privilege that he /she is chosen by Christ with a capacity to be *fruitful*. So he/she

---

[177] The Holy Spirit is the "parakletos," the divine counsellor, helper and encourager as explained earlier, also in MacArthur, (2005), pages 80-82.

is not useless in the community. They are chosen for a purpose to serve God.

5.  These things I have spoken to you, that My *joy* may remain in you, and that your joy may be full." Joy comes from having been through difficulties, trials and dark times, and discovering that God is faithful.

6.  John 15:13 says, "Greater *love* has no one than this, than to lay down one's life for his friends." Loving obedience is the motivation of the counselee's life.

7.  John 15:2 says, "Every branch in Me that does not bear fruit He takes away; and every branch that bears fruit He prunes, that it may bear more fruit." God disciplines His children. Painful experience can have a positive purpose.

Dye ends up by saying that encouragers lift people up when they are down. They remind the sufferers that the Vinedresser is in the midst of their pain and He is working to achieve His ultimate goal that will be both pleasing and fruitful.

Diagram 3 :  **Level  II  Counseling (Exhortation)[1]**

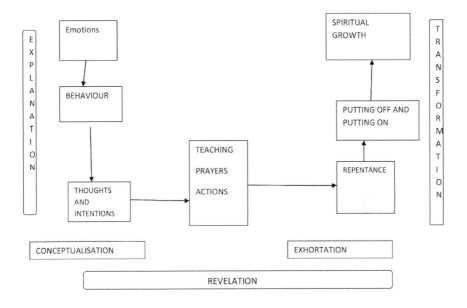

[1] Colin Dye Book, "Loving Obedience" page 88

## Colin Dye's Level II Counseling (Manual Two)
## An Outline of Counseling Level II of Dye's model [178]

Dye (2013) says some problems or difficulties cannot be solved by just encouraging the counselee. The counselee might need a formal way of counseling which is why Dye wrote his second manual. It deals with the correction of the counselee's behavior from problem behavior to biblical behavior (Exhortation). Mature members like elders, pastors and other responsible people in the church, could be trained for level II. But a few selected individuals could be trained for Level III Counseling where they can deal with more complicated and stubborn problems. [179]

According to Dye, there are three main stages in the formal Level II Counseling process: The early stage (exploration), the middle stage (revelation) and the final stage (transformation). Each stage has particular objectives and calls for particular skills (Diagram 3).

1.  Exploration stage or early stage (2-4 sessions): this stage examines the problem in its three dimensions: emotions, behavior, and thoughts. The aim is to move to a particular analysis or conceptualization. Dye repeats what Crabb mentions on this issue, that the human being strives for security and significance. Once these essential elements are threatened, negative emotions like anger, fear or anxiety, sadness, guilt and vague feelings of emptiness emerge,[180] with subsequent problems in behavior. The counselor should go

---

[178] Colin Dye, *Loving Obedience, Basic Biblical Counselling.* (London, UK: KT publications, 2013) 88-115.

[179] This idea is originally taken from Crabb's book, "Effective Biblical Counselling." pp 165-191

[180] The 5 main negative emotions are already mentioned by Crabb with little modification, as Dye replaces resentment with anger.

into depth[181] as how the up-bringing of the counselee could have attributed to the present problem, also how the counselee's circles of life like health, occupation, marriage, finance, sexuality, and so forth, led to or were affected by the presenting problem. However for the biblical Counselor, it is important to explore whether the problem is caused by ignorance of biblical teaching, or not. [182] This stage is completed by the formulation of the problem with a plan of a realistic goal (conceptualization). This should be understood and agreed by the counselee.

2. Revelation or middle stage (8-10 sessions): this stage starts with conceptualization and ends with exhortation. It is the core stage of counseling. During these sessions, the counselor teaches from the Bible, prays with the counselee and directs him/her to a suggested plan of action to solve the problems in line with the Scripture, in a mutual, collaborative effort.

1. Transformation or final stage (2-4 sessions): this stage starts with exhortation or re-enforcement of changes that have been introduced in the counselee's life until the new ways of biblical thinking and behaving are thoroughly internalized. The counselor should avoid the counselee's dependence on him or her in solving other emerging problems. When the goal is achieved, the interval between sessions is gradually increased, with a final session of follow up around 3-6 months thereafter. The goal of this stage is

---

[181] These elements of deeper issues are discussed in Welsh article "Are You Feeling Inadequate, A Letter to Biblical Counsellor" The Journal of Biblical Counselling volume 26/ number 3 pp 6-17 CCEF publisher.

[182] It is also needed to explore what the counselee has done to solve the problem. Sometimes he/ she comes for biblical counselling as a last resort after exhausting other options, for example level one counselling, psychology, psychiatry input, and so forth.

spiritual growth with repentance, putting off unbiblical behaviors and putting on the biblical ones, according to Ephesians 4:22-24. [183]

## Comments on Dye's Level II Counseling (Manual Two)

1. Dye modifies Crabb's model in this way: instead of the seven stages of Crabb's, he reduces them to only three stages. He condensed the first three stages which are: identify problem feelings, identifying problem behavior, and identify problem thinking to one stage of exploration. The middle stage of Dye (exhortation) replaces stage 4 (clarify biblical thinking) and stage 5 (secure commitment). Dye's final stage of transformation corresponds to stage 6 (plan and carry out biblical behavior) and stage 7 (identify Spirit –controlled feelings).

2. Dye is affected by secular psychology to the extent that he avoids the biblical terms of "sin" or "sinful behavior". Instead he puts a vague term of "repentance" in his final stage of counseling without explaining what this repentance is for.

3. In his final stage, Dye replaces the "Tape Recorder" technique of Crabb's, with Adams' main idea of change which is "Putting off – Putting on" maybe because the latter has a biblical basis in Ephesians 4:22-24.

---

[183] Dye takes this idea from Adams model, although he does not acknowledge that in his manual.

## The Fruit and the Gifts of the Holy Spirit in Dye's Level II Counseling

Dye does not ignore the Holy Spirit completely, as Crabb does. For example, Dye refers to the Holy Spirit, when he talks about the resources available for the counselee in Christ, by saying:

> God has not left us helpless, alone or abandoned as orphans. Christ has given us "another comforter", the Holy Spirit, who is the divine Paraclete,[184] called by Jesus to be alongside us as our constant helper, companion and friend. He continually administers to us the empowering and enabling presence of the Lord.[185]

Dye goes further by saying that the Christian counselors should seek to use the charismatic gifts of the Holy Spirit, mentioned in 1 Corinth. 12. The gifts of revelation: prophecy, word of knowledge, word of wisdom and discerning the spirits are especially useful for the counselors. However, Dye does not elaborate further and says there are guidelines to explain that, but he refrains from giving references for that.

## Conclusion

In 2012, Colin Dye planned to publish three counseling manuals to lay a foundation for the counseling ministry in the church. These manuals (three levels of counseling, one book for each level) are intended to take the would-be counselor on a journey from the basics of biblical counseling to more advanced level. Dye adopted these counseling manuals from

---

[184] In Crabb's model, the word "Paraclete" is used to describe the characters of the human biblical counsellor, as outlined earlier, ignoring the Holy Spirit, the divine counsellor.

[185] Colin Dye, Loving Obedience, Basic Biblical Counselling, (London, UK: KT publication,2013)127.

Larry Crabb's integration model of counseling in his book, "Effective Biblical Counseling," published in 1977. Level I Counseling deals with "Encouragement," where a believer encourages another believer who has difficulty or problem. Although not mentioned in the original Crabb's model, Dye highlights the importance of the Holy Spirit and His fruit, especially joy and love in this Level I Counseling. This kind of counseling does not require formal training and it can be done causally when the counselor meets the counselee at church or in small circle worship like home groups.

For Level II Counseling which deals with "Exhortation," the correction of the behavior of the counselees, Dye develops a structured model, adopted from the integration model of Crabb. There is no mention of the fruit and the gifts of the Spirit in the core elements of this model. However, Dye talks about the importance of the Holy Spirit as a divine resource for the counselee and the charismatic gifts of the Holy Spirit, especially the gifts of revelation, as helping tools for the counselors. Dye did not publish the third manual, as planned, which deals with the change of thinking of the counselees; the reason for that is not clear.

# Chapter Six

# THE MUSTARD SEED MODEL OF BIBLICAL COUNSELING

This model that I have developed is not new. It is based on the foundation that already been established by biblical counselors like Jay Adams, John MacArthur, Colin Dye and others. The materials have been gathered from more than 10 year study of biblical counseling from a Master degree to the Doctorate degree, and from my experience working in the field of psychiatry for more than 17 years. Most importantly, I have been sensitive to the Holy Spirit, who gave me ideas while I was working through my final project of my Ph.D and also reminded me with the verses of the Scripture related to the topics which are the concern of this study.[186]

However, the unique thing about this model is that it is based entirely on the fruit of the Holy Spirit, such as is mentioned in Galatians 5:22-23 and His supernatural charismatic gifts, recorded in 1 Corinthians 12: 1-11, as well as the Word of God in the Scripture, which is the sword of the Spirit as explained in Ephesians 6:17.

---

[186] Mark and Patti Virkler, *Counselled by God, Emotional Wholeness by Hearing God's voice*, (Shippensburg, PA: Destiny Image Publishers) 1-8.

The name of the Model is taken from what the Lord Jesus says in Mathew 17[187] and also in Luke 17[188]. The Mustard Seed of faith which is implanted by the Spirit at salvation grows up when watered by the Spirit and nourished by the Word of God to produce fruit. The same Mustard Seed of faith grows further to move mountains and pull up the mulberry trees of guilt, resentment, anger, and so forth, that have been rooted for years in the mind and the soul of the counselees as the result of accumulated, overwhelming problems in their lives either because of their sins or simply because we live in a fallen world.

However, before going further to discuss the stages of the model, and to get the full picture of the counseling process, I would like to highlight the following principles related to biblical counseling. Most of these are taken from Jay Adams' books of CtC and Christian Counseling manual or elsewhere in other counseling manuals:

1.  **The Human counselors**: Adams[189] writes about the character and qualification of the counselor. He also mentions the gifts of pastoral ministry which are required for biblical counselors.[190] For this model to be effective, the counselors should be filled with the Holy Spirit and strive to have the supernatural gifts mentioned in 1 Corinthians 12:1-11 especially the gifts of revelation: the word of wisdom, the word of knowledge, and prophecy, as been discussed earlier when examining Colin Dye's Level II counseling model.

---

[187] Mathew 17:20.

[188] Luke 17:6

[189] Adams' Manual pp 9-20.

[190] We can notice here that he does not mention the supernatural gifts recoded in 1 Cornth1-11, as he believes that, these gifts were ceased by the end time of the apostles of the early church, as explained earlier.

2. **The Counselees**: A lot has been written about the counselees in Adams' Manual,[191] but what should be stressed here is that they should be saved or born again Christians . The counselors should be assured of that. It is the first step of the early stage of this counseling model.

3. **The setting:** All biblical counselors agree that the counseling ministry should be part of the ministry of the Church,[192] where the counselors are members. They should be supervised by the pastors or elders of these churches. As a general rule, a woman should counsel a woman, a man counsels another man, and a couple counsel (not necessary husband and wife) a couple, unless in special circumstances, when the same sex counselor is not available but this should be with the agreement of the church.

4. **Fee for the service:** Some biblical counselors charges for the service, but I believe this is not a biblical principle. Biblical counseling is a ministry of the church and the church should not charge fees for their ministries. However, expenses like hiring an outside venue (when there is no room is available at church) or paying for bills such as water and electricity, cost money, so the counselors should explain that to the counselees, and it is up to them if they want to contribute by donation for the service to continue.

5. **The number, duration, and the frequency of sessions:**[193] Most biblical counselors agree that the average number of sessions is 12 sessions, one hour on a weekly basis. This number can be less or more, but the counselors should avoid discharging the counselees prematurely, also avoid the counselees' dependence on them for

---

[191] Adams's Manual, pp 21-30.

[192] Besides the two references of Adams above, it is also mentioned in details in his book, "A Theology of Biblical Counselling." pp 276-296

[193] This also been highlighted in Dye's book, level II counselling manual when discussing his model pp89-115

solving every problem in their lives. When the counseling sessions are about to finish, the interval between sessions can be increased gradually to fortnightly then every three weeks. Contact between the counselors and the counselees should be avoided between sessions unless in emergency. At the end of the counseling when the goal is achieved, a follow- up session in three to four month time will be arranged. Asking the counselees to join lively bible-based churches is part of the counseling process.

6. **Confidentiality:** Dye[194] stresses that the counselees should be assured that everything they say will remain confidential.[195] Counselees should keep records of the weekly counseling sessions. The counselors should also do that but for the sake of confidentiality, they keep the files anonymous, to be identified by letters or numbers.[196]

7. **Homework:** As part of the process, after each counseling session, the Counselors [197]should assign homework. There are many advantages of that, recorded in Adams', and Dye's manuals.

---

[194] Dye's book "Ministry in the Spirit."Page 167.

[195] In special circumstances when a counselee or other people lives are in danger, the counsellor is obliged by law to diverge information to other parties, but this should be discussed first with the pastor of the church.

[196] Keeping records with confidentially are also discussed in details in Eyrich' book, " Curing the Hearts" pp171-176

[197] Also in Eyrich's book, "Curing the Heart" pp151-160.

Diagram 4: **Mustard Seed Model of Biblical Counseling**[1]

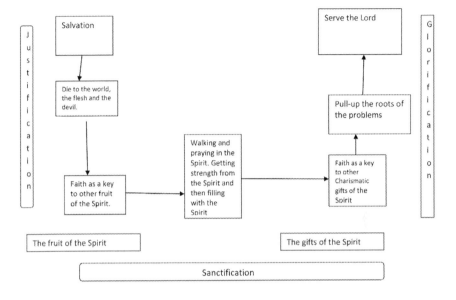

---

[1] The name is taken from the Lord Jesus' words in Mathew 17:20 about the mustard seed of faith that moves the mountain, also His words in Luke 17:6, about the same mustard seed of faith that pulls up the roots of mulberry tree, and orders it to be planted in the sea.

# An Outline of the Mustard Seed
# Model of Biblical Counseling

As in diagram 4, the model is composed of three stages: Early stage of justification, middle stage of sanctification and the final stage of glorification. Each stage has two steps, so there are 6 steps in total in the model.

## 1. Early Stage of Justification:

Step one, salvation: the counselor should be assured that the counselee is converted or born-again Christian. If not or he/she is not sure, the counselor should explain the salvation as the gift of the Holy Spirit, we take it by grace[198]. He then invites the counselee to receive it. The Mustard Seed of faith is then implanted into the soul of the counselee, when he/she prays this prayer aloud:

> **Dear Lord Jesus. I am a sinner. I do believe that you died and rose from the dead to save me from my sins. I want to be with you in heaven forever. God, forgive me of all my sins that I have committed against you. I, here and now, open my heart to you and ask you to come to my heart and life and be my personal Savior. Amen.[199]**

When the counselee prays the sinner's prayer and means it, he is now a child of God and he has been transferred from the devil's dominion to

---

[198] As explained before, salvation is entirely the *work* of the Holy Spirit, in the sense that the person who receives it does not need to do good deeds or improve his/herself, just be open to the Spirit.

[199] Lester Sumrall, *The Gifts and Ministries of the Holy Spirit* (South Bend, IN: Whitaker House Publication,1982)267

the kingdom of God. The homework that can be assigned at the end of this session may be from 1 John 1:9 and Colossians 1:13.

Step two, die to the world, the flesh and the devil: this is the next step the counselee should do as the key for change. Romans 5:11 says, "Likewise you also, reckon yourselves to be *dead* indeed to sin, but alive to God in Christ Jesus our Lord." The result is the change recorded in verse 12, "Therefore do not let sin reign in your *mortal* body, that you should obey it in lusts."

**2. Middle Stage of Sanctification:** this is the main stage of counseling. During this stage, the fruit and the charismatic gifts of the Holy Spirit are emphasized while dealing with the counselee's problems or difficulties he seeks counseling for. However like any counseling process, the counselor gathers data, writes a tentative formulation with a goal of counseling and a plan of how to proceed further. The Spirit filled counselor always asks the Holy Spirit in prayer to give him the word of wisdom, the word of knowledge and prophesy (the revelation gifts). The goal here is not only solving the counselee's problems or difficulties of life in line with God's word and will, but also asking God to use these situations to prepare him for serving the Lord.[200]

Step three, faith as the key to other fruit[201] of the Spirit[202]: now the ground is ready for sowing. The counselee is sure of his salvation.[203] He agrees to repent of all his sinful behavior and works of the flesh and is ready

---

[200] Colin Dye's book, *Ministry in the Spirit* (London, UK: KT publications, 2007), 162-163.

[201] Galatians 5:22-23, the concern of this study, as outlined earlier.

[202] Timothy Lane (2006), *how people change*. He has developed a model which depends only on the fruit by focusing on Christ (but he does not specify the fruit of the Holy Spirit). His whole model is based on the fruit of the believers, in contrast to the thorns; they used to bear before coming to Christ. Illustration,100.

[203] There will be a sense of peace when he feels all his sins are forgiven and he is now a new creation in Christ..But Satan sometimes makes him doubt. In this case he is armed with the Spirit' Sword, the Word of God, for example 1 John 1:9.

to move forward in his relation with God, by sowing in the Spirit. The goal of this stage is to conform to Jesus' likeness in character and behavior, in other words to pursue sanctification.

According to Adams, the sanctification stage is unlike justification, where the Holy Spirit does the entire job of planting and cultivating the mustard seed of faith; here, the Holy Spirit *enables* the counselee to pursue the *fruit* of the Spirit. But how that can be achieved?

Referring to Ezekiel, chapter 47 of the vision of the Water/ the Holy Spirit comes down the south of the Altar (the Calvary-cost of redemption), the counselor explains to the counselee the four measures for fullness of the Holy Spirit [204]as follows:

A) Water to the ankles, walk in the Spirit: Paul gives this command to the Galatians, "Walk in the Spirit and you will not fulfill the desires of the flesh"(Galatians 5:16). It is important to understand that we still have fleshly desires. These negative influences pull us away from God. It is important to understand how the flesh operates in people's lives. Damaged emotions, past hurts and demonic powers continue to have a negative effect on us. They are often at the root of many of counseling problems. Walking in the Spirit gives us the power to live free with Abba Father. But how can we achieve that? It is by studying the Bible, obeying God's commands, attending regular worships and cutting out all sinful temptations. Adams calls the latter, "radical amputation" and includes it as part of the doctrine of sanctification,[205] where the counselee is instructed by the counselor to delete all links with sin, for examples, telephone numbers, adult websites on the internet or TV channels, also cut relationships with all bad friends who are

---

[204] As explained early, the Holy Spirit dwells in the believer once he/she is saved or converted.

[205] Jay E Adams book,*A Theology of Christian Counselling* (Grand Rapids, MI: Zondervan, 1979)163-166.

tempting him/her to sin. It is not Adams' idea but it is the Lord Jesus who commands this in Mathew 5:29-30.[206] In this context, the Apostle Paul argues with the believers, "And do not grieve the Holy Spirit of God (by sin)[207] by whom you were sealed for the day of redemption" (Ephesians 4:30).

B) Waters to the knee, prayer in the Spirit: Here it is not meant to be a regular traditional prayer, although it is important, but it is a prayer empowered by the Spirit. The counselee may come for counseling because of a life-threatening problem or crisis. So he needs to be aware of God's empowering presence in his situation or problem. The counselor should explain to the counselee that the barrier of sin is broken. God is glad to hear from his children and His door is wide open 24 hours/7 days a week.

The role of the Holy Spirit here is to provide help in prayer. Derek Prince (1977)[208] says there are four means of such help. First, Romans 8:26-27[209], the Apostle Paul says, "The Holy Spirit Himself makes *intercession* for us with groaning which cannot be uttered." Second, Romans 12:2, and Ephesians 4:23, the Apostle Paul says the Holy Spirit *illuminates* our minds in prayer.[210] Third, the Holy Spirit *puts the right words* in our mouth.[211]

---

[206] Obviously Jesus does not mean literally to pluck out one's eye in verse 29, or amputate one's right hand in verse 30, but He means the counselees to have a strong stand against all things that cause temptation to sin.

[207] Sin in the lives of the believer is exception, as we still have the old nature. If it happens, we need to repent, Psalm 51 is famous in this context.

[208] Derek Prince, *The Spirit in You* (Charloote, NC: Whitaker House,1977)65-72.

[209] Gordon Fee in his book, *God Empowering Presence* says, whether Paul means prayer in tongues, but it is not clear from this verse. pp581-583

[210] Many Christians record experience while they prayed in the Spirit for a solution for a particular problem, suddenly the Holy Spirit illuminated their minds about how to sort out the problem in a way they kept wondering why they did not think about this solution before.

[211] One of the gifts of the Holy Spirit is to give us the word of knowledge in the sense we pray about something, although by our natural abilities, there is no evidence it is happening. We

Fourth, He gives us a new unknown language in prayer, or praying in *tongues.*

C) Waters to the loins, strength by the Spirit: Here the Lord Jesus says to his disciples, "Behold, I send the promise of My Father upon you: but tarry in the city of Jerusalem until you are endued with *power* from high" (Luke 24:49). This divine power is needed to strengthen the counselee while dealing with his problems or difficulties in life.

D) Waters to swim, the fullness of the Holy Spirit: Acts 2:4, says at the day of Pentecost, after they prayed, "And they were all filled with the Holy Spirit and began to speak with other tongues, as the Spirit gave them utterance." Referring to what was explained earlier, the baptism of the Holy Spirit occurs once at conversion, but the fillings are many. It is God's command to be filled with the Spirit.[212] It can be continuous but also can occur in a crisis situation, where the counselee needs the Holy Spirit to be manifested in his problem or situation. The filling with the Spirit opens the door to the gifts of the Spirit, which is the next step of this counseling model

Step 4 of the model: The same mustard seed of faith, that was implanted at salvation by the Holy Spirit and was the key for the fruit in Galatians 5:22-23, in step 3, here "faith" is among the charismatic gifts of the Spirit in 1 Corinthians 12:1-11. This mustard seed of faith now does supernatural works after having been nourished with the filing of the Holy Spirit. It moves mountains in Math. 17, and pulls up the roots of the problems in

---

then discover later that it was the case and our prayers made all the difference.

[212] Ephesians 5:18.

Luke 17.The counselor should urge the counselee to "eagerly desire" these gifts (1Cornthins 12:31 and 1 Corinthians 14:1).

In this context, Dye[213] explains further by saying that counseling in the Spirit, like other ministries of the Spirit, revolves around the charismatic gifts recorded in 1 Corinthians 12:1-11. In verse 7, these gifts are given to each one for the profit of all. Dye looks at the word "given" in Greek language, *didomi*. It means these gifts are given continuously.[214] Also these gifts are given to the believers to do things beyond their natural abilities and their previous training.

According to Dye, these gifts flow from the believers to others.[215] In counseling, they flow from the counselors to the counselees in a supernatural way. Dye uses medical term by saying they are infectious.[216] This is marvelous! When a counselor has the gift of the word of wisdom, for example, this word of wisdom could be transferred to a counselee, so he/she may use this gift to counsel others in the Spirit.

**3. The Final stage of Glorification:** during this stage, the counselor is prepared to end the counseling sessions as the goal of sanctification is in progress[217] and the counselee reaches a satisfactory solution to his problem. Now it is the time to celebrate and glorify the Lord. The Apostle Paul says

---

[213] Dye's book, "Ministry in the Spirit" page 162.

[214] Given continuously in the sense that they are still been given and never ceased as some theologians say.

[215] The Lord Jesus says in John 4:14," But the water(the Holy Spirit) that I shall give him (the believer) will become a fountain of water springing up into everlasting life."

[216] The same expression of "infectious" is used by Gordon Fee when he explains that the likeness of God infected the saved person at the time of conversion, manifested in the fruit of the Spirit as outlined before.

[217] Progressive sanctification is a life-long process to be like Jesus will end in Heaven when we meet Jesus face to face. But the important thing now in counselling is to let the counselee start and make progress in this process.

about Abraham, the man of faith in Romans 4:20,[218] "He did not waver at the promise of God through unbelief, but was strengthened in *faith*, giving *glory* to God." However, before ending the counseling sessions, there are a couple of important issues which need final attention.

Step 5, Pull up the roots of negative emotions: the roots of long years of bitterness, resentment, guilt, anxiety, and so forth, carry deep emotional wounds, difficult to heal, even after all the work that has been done in counseling. These need to be cleared up, for the counselee to feel the full peace of Christ.

In this context, the psychiatric disorders classification, DSM-IV-TR (2000)[219] describes a condition where a person may come for therapy because he experienced, witnessed, or was confronted with an event that involved actual or threatened death or serious injury. This person developed a sense of intense fear, helplessness or horror at that time. Later, he might sustain what is called "Post-traumatic stress disorder," or PTSD, with recurrent intense psychological distress at exposure to similar situation. He has developed flashbacks and distressing dreams as the consequence. Andrew Sims (1999)[220] says that this condition is difficult to be treated with psychotherapy or medication, so he suggests hypnosis.[221]

Whether a counselee seeks counseling because of the deep negative emotions or PTSD, he needs the charismatic gift of "healings" to heal his

---

[218] Abraham was in a difficult situation, he was about 100 years of age and his wife Sarah was 90 years with no children, but by faith in God's promises, he got his son Isaac.

[219] DSM-IV-TR (QUICK REFERENCE) pp 218-220

[220] Andrew Sims, *Symptoms in the Mind, An Introduction to Descriptive Psycho-pathology*, (London, UK: W.B Saunders Company LTD)45-47

[221] The person comes to an agreement with the therapist to have some sort of amnesia/loss of memory of a particular painful event happened in the past, then the hypnotist does certain procedure to achieve this goal, the same reference above page 46. Whether this method is biblical or unbiblical is beyond the scope of this study.

memories. The roots need to be pulled up, and planted in the sea.[222] The counselee still remembers the experience, but that past cannot stir up his negative disturbing emotions and will not disturb his peace and quietness in the Lord.

Step 6: Serving the Lord. It is the final step and part of this model, so it is not an option but a must. There are many ways to serve the Lord. One of the most common ways in this context is the counselees become counselors. For example, the former drug addict becomes a support worker in the local church, preaching the gospel and helping other drug addicts to enjoy the freedom and sobriety he has now in Christ. In John 8:36, the Lord Jesus says, "Therefore if the Son makes you free, you shall be free indeed."

## Practical Application

A British woman, Jackie Pullinger travelled from England to Hong Kong in 1966. She had no idea that God was calling her to the Walled City- a notorious, sprawling warren of slums, rats, gangsters and drug addicts in the Kowloon district. Yet as she spoke of Jesus Christ, brutal triad gangsters were converted, prostitutes left their lifestyle and Jackie discovered a new treatment for drug addiction: baptism in the Holy Spirit. Her success inspired me in formulating this Mustard Seed model which depends entirely on the fruit and the charismatic gifts of the Holy Spirit.

R.T. Kendall[223] travelled to Hong Kong to preach there and he met her in the late 1980s. Jackie explained to him that her ministry was almost totally aimed at heroin addicts in the streets of Hong Kong. Her method was to tell them about Jesus who died for their sins and rose from the dead,

[222] The metaphor of the mulberry tree in Luke 17:6, "be pulled up by the roots and be planted in the sea" signifies that it will not come to the surface again; this is the miraculous work of the mustard seed of faith.

[223] R.T. Kendall, *The HolyFire, A Balanced, Biblical Look At The Holy Spirit's Work In Our Lives* (Lake Mary, Florida: Charisma House, 2004)140-143.

and that He is the Son of God and they need to receive Him. Some of them, she said, were so near death that they could barely speak. That did not stop her. She would give them the Gospel and ask them to believe in Jesus Christ- that He is the Son of God. As soon as they prayed the sinner's prayer she then told them, "Now start speaking in a language not your own." They had no biases of any kind and dutifully did just that-speaking in an unknown language. They spoke in tongues and then they came off heroin, day after day.

Kendall comments on that by saying that she did what hospitals, psychiatrists and psychologists had failed to do. The city of Hong Kong eventually gave Jackie acres of property to do her missionary work. The skeptical BBC did a documentary about her and found her work to be genuine and the results unexaggerated. She was awarded the coveted OBE (Order of the British Empire) by Her Majesty the Queen.

Jackie Pullinger (2001) writes about an American charismatic sailor who accompanied her on a walk around the Walled City for a day while they were praying in tongues. He had this charismatic gift but he thought that Jackie made too much of it. During that day they prayed continually in tongues only stopping when they were eating.

Here is part of that day:

As we left the den we were followed by Ah Wing, a mean man who sold heroin, killing others' bodies as well as his own. He came to eat noodles with us, through no good motives at all – he just wanted a free meal. I was telling him about Jesus and he was hurrying this bit through to get the noodles.

"Are you willing to believe that Jesus is the Son Of God?" I asked him. "I am not sure," he replied, "Maybe."

I did not think he was that convinced but I went on to the next question.

"And do you believe that He died for you?"

"Don't understand that."

"Well, never mind, are you willing?"

"All right," he mumbled.

"Are you willing to believe that He rose again from the dead?"

"I suppose He must have," he acquiesced, "because I have heard about things He is doing."

"Are you willing to follow Him?"

He answered scathingly. "Oh yes. I mean if he is true God, of course."

"Ah Wing, why don't you ask God if Jesus is His Son or not? I am sure He will let you know."

I suggested and began to pray quietly, motioning the American to join us.

As we prayed there at the noodle stall, Ah Wing joined in with us gently and confidently in tongues.

Two more people were converted later on our walk and my American friend needed no more convincing about praying in the Spirit.[224]

## Case Study

This case study is a real life scenario of a 68 year old man, admitted to the psychiatric hospital because he wanted to kill himself. There was NO mental illness. He received input from the psychiatric service but with no improvement.[225]

- The 68 year old man was admitted to the psychiatric ward
- Reason of admission: he went for his fourth session of CBT (Cognitive Behaviour Therapy) with IAPT (a secular psychology

---

[224] Jackie Pullinger and Andrew Quickie, *Chasing the Dragon,* (London, UK: Hodder &Stoughton Ltd, 2001)227-228.

[225] This case study was presented by me in a psychiatric conference in Feb. 2013, under the topic of "Spirituality and Psychiatry." The names and location are kept anonymous for confidentiality. The management of this case as outlined here in this study was not part of the presentation.

setting). He confessed to them that he had been suicidal, wanting to kill himself, so he was referred for admission.

- When he was seen by the psychiatrist, he told him about his traumatic life experience and how he was the only child of his parents who owned a farm and how they abused him emotionally and physically,

- They ignored his education, forced him to work long hours, treated him like an animal on the farm.

- At the age of 18, he managed to escape to work as a labourer in a nearby farm. His parents replaced him with a stranger and they did not want him back.

- He worked as a cheap labourer on that farm for around 25 years. He heard that his parents had died, and the stranger they hired possessed the farm and did not give him any inheritance.

- He then managed to work as a carrier for the Royal Mail and he immersed himself in work for another 25 years, trying to forget his painful past

- Recently, he was forced to retire from the Royal Mail. He moved to his current retirement bedsit in another city, looking for a fresh start in his new location.

- He tried to forget his past and to become a "religious" person. He attended a local church and received a brief counselling from the pastor there.[226] However his condition got worse. Now he is angry towards God blaming Him for allowing him to suffer. He stops going to churches. Now he is on medication for depression besides the psychotherpay but with no improvement.

So, how does a biblical counselor manage similar cases by applying the "Mustard Seed" model of biblical counseling? Two important issues

---

[226] He said he attended a local church a couple of times and the pastor of that church visited him a couple of times in his flat.

need to be considered, while allowing the Holy Spirit to take control on the counseling agenda.

1. Step one of the model is mandatory. He should be saved by praying the sinner's prayer above, accepting Jesus as the Savior. The model depends entirely on the Holy Spirit, who dwells only in believers as I explained earlier.

2. Once step one is completed, the counselor should be open to the Holy Spirit. The Holy Spirit needs to have full control. This means the counselor should not be obliged to follow the order of the steps in the model. The counselor may ask the counselee to speak in another language, straightforward, after being saved like Pullinger's cases mentioned above (speaking in tongues is one of the charismatic gifts of the Holy Spirit: step 4 of the model).[227]

**Early Stage of Justification:**

1. Step one, Salvation: the counselor should first explain to him that his suffering is not directly related to his sins and we cannot blame God for allowing his parents to abuse him. Something wrong like this can happen in our fallen world. Because of the sin of Adam and Eve, sin entered the world. Shortly after that, Cain killed his brother without real reason.[228] That is why Jesus came to the world, to save those who believe in Him from the consequences of sin and to give eternal life for those who believe.[229] Romans 5:1 say, "Therefore, having been justified by

---

[227] Kenneth Hagin insists that the newly born Christian, after conversion should speak and pray in tongues, as a prove of being saved; Kenneth Hagin, *7 Vital Steps to Receiving the Holy Spirit* (Toronto, Ontario: Rhema Church publication,1980) 51-52. However there is no evidence in the Scripture to support this claim.

[228] Genesis 4.

[229] John 3:16

faith, we have peace with God through our Lord Jesus Christ." So the counselor should explain to the counselee that he should have peace with God through salvation first. The peace of God spreads to peace with self which then spreads to peace with others. Repentance of sin is part of salvation. He needs to repent for the "hidden" sin of unforgiveness.[230] This man endures a deep sense of resentment towards his parents, which is understandable, but he needs to change, and this change of feelings cannot be achieved without repentance. It is difficult, but again, this is the work of the Holy Spirit, not the work of man. In this context, Joel Green (2008)[231]emphasizes that repentance in the Bible represents *a fundamental change in thinking* which enables diverse individuals to receive salvation and become children of God.

2.  Step two: Die to the world, flesh and the devil. This man needs to realize and believe that he is now a new man in Christ according to, 2 Corinthians 5:17, "Therefore if anyone in Christ, he is a new creation; old things have passed away; behold, all things have become new."

**Middle Stage of Sanctification:**

3.  Step three: faith as a key to other fruit of the Spirit: true faith or trusting God expresses itself in Love. In other words faith, here the mustard seed, is a key to the other fruitage of the Spirit mentioned in Galatians 5:22-23, namely joy, peace, longsuffering, kindness, goodness, gentleness, and self control. In this case, joy and peace in love are most needed. According to Adams, this counselee should *pursue* or strive to get this fruit, empowered by the Holy Spirit

---

[230] Repentance of un-forgiveness, is for his sake first to relief his bitterness and resentment towards his late parents.

[231] Joel B Green, *Body, Soul, and Human Life* (Grand Rapids, MI: BakerAcademic, 2008)11.

who already dwells in him in salvation. Dye uses the same idea but in a different way, that the counselee should sow this cluster of fruit. How can that be done? The answer is recorded earlier, by walking, praying in the Spirit, getting strength and being filled with the Spirit. [232] Both Crabb and Dye record that it is not that easy. Years of resentment, sufferings and bitterness would not go away overnight. It is hard work as it is beyond this man's natural ability. However there is hope. The divine help from the Holy Spirit is available. So he can say with the Apostle Paul in Romans 8:37, "Yet in all these things we are more than conqueror through Him who loved me."

4. Step 4: Faith as a key to other gifts of the Spirit: Here the mustard seed of faith, *pistis,* that was originally implanted in step one by salvation, has grown up to bring the fruit of the Spirit in step 3, grows further, to bring the other supernatural gifts of the Holy Spirit of 1 Corinthians 12:1-11, namely the word of wisdom, the word of knowledge, healings, miracles, prophecy, discerning the spirits, different kinds of tongues, and interpretation of tongues. This man needs healing of his memories, which is the gift of the Holy Spirit. The counselor should pray with him for this gift. The best example in the Bible is Joseph. He suffered a lot from his brothers who were jealous of him and they wanted to kill him but instead they sold him as a slave. When Joseph became the second man of Egypt after the Pharaoh, the Bible teaches us that he forgave and forgot what his brothers had done for him, and

---

[232] The Lord Jesus mentions also in Mathew 17:21 that "this kind of spirit (the evil spirit that possessed the boy in that story)does not go out except by prayer and fasting." Here to stress that some stubborn problems cannot be solved except by fasting. Fasting in this case is important to concentrate on prayer and meditation in the Scripture, asking the Holy Spirit to intervene in the problem or difficulty.

when he had his first born son he named him "Manaseh"[233] as he said, "For God has made me *forget* all my toil and all my father's house"(Genesis 41:51).

**Final Stage of Glorification:**

5.  Step 5, Pull-up the roots of the problems. That is marvelous, according to the Lord Jesus' words in Luke 17, "If you have faith as a mustard seed, you can say to this mulberry tree, 'Be pulled up by the roots and be planted in the sea,' and it would obey you." All the negative emotions of this man: bitterness, resentment, hurt, anger, and so forth, as the result of his years of sufferings will vanish. He may remember these things, but that would no longer disturb his peace, quietness, and the joy of having the relationship with the Lord.

6.  Step 6, Serve the Lord: serving the Lord comes naturally as the result of the above steps. It is part of sowing and reaping the fruit and the gifts of the Holy Spirit. It should be part of this man's life, something to live for, to give him value and purpose.

---

[233] A Hebrew name means literally making forgetful.

# Chapter 7

# CONCLUSIONS

In this study, I examined the benefits of the fruit and the charismatic gifts of the Holy Spirit in counseling Christian believers biblically, with reference to three scholars: Jay Adams, Gordon Fee, and Colin Dye. The fruit of the Spirit is recorded in Galatians 5:22-23,"But the fruit of the Spirit is love, joy, peace, longsuffering, kindness, goodness, faithfulness, gentleness, self control. Against such there is no law. " The charismatic gifts are mentioned in 1 Corinthians 12:8-10: the word of wisdom, the word of knowledge, faith, healings, miracles, prophecy, discerning of spirits, different kinds of tongues and interpretation of tongues.

Jay Adams has developed his own model of biblical counseling, known as Nouthetic Counseling, based on the confrontation of sins to achieve the change required in feelings, behavior, and thoughts of the counselees. So, I studied the role of the fruit and the charismatic gifts of the Holy Spirit in his model. I did the same with Colin Dye's model of counseling. However, Dye adopted the integration model (the integration of Christian faith with secular psychology) of Larry Crabb, the well-known Christian psychologist, with some modification as explained in the study.

Most of the materials that I have been studied for Adams were taken from his two famous books, "Competent to Counsel" and "Christian

Counseling Manual," besides his book "A Theology of Christian Counseling." For Dye, most of the materials were taken from his two counseling manuals, Counseling Level I and II. Dye planned to write the third manual of level III counseling, but the latter book has never come to light. The reason for that is not known.

Gordon Fee was also included in the study. Although he has no counseling model of his own, like the other two scholars, his scholarly comments on the fruit and the charismatic gifts of the Holy Spirit enriched my understanding and added another dimension to the study. The materials were taken from his two books, "Paul, the Spirit and the People of God," and "God's Empowering Presence."

I summarize the results as follows:

1.  On one hand, Adams insists that we cannot counsel unbelievers in the biblical sense of the word (changing them, sanctifying them through the work of the Holy Spirit, as His Word is ministered to their hearts), so long as they remain unbelievers. If the unbelievers want to come for biblical counseling, they should have one or two sessions of evangelism with the counselors first.

2.  On the other hand, Dye, because he adopts Crabb's model, has no objection to counseling unbelievers, as he says they should be counseled in a different way according to their way of life, with an ultimate aim of leading them to Christ.

3.  Adams examines the fruit of the Holy Spirit, the nine folds of Galatians 5:22-23 above, but he adds three items from 1Timothy 6:11 and 2Timothy 2:22 which are righteousness, godliness and endurance. He concludes that they come in a singular cluster of "fruit" and it has a crucial role in his counseling model. It can change the personality trait of the counselees with a view to conforming them to Jesus likeness. The fruit of the Spirit is part of the process of progressive sanctification which should be the ultimate goal of biblical counseling. The counselors should help

the counselees to put off the works of the flesh and to put on the fruit of the Spirit. The sanctification process, unlike salvation which is entirely the work of the Holy Spirit, needs the counselees to pursue this Spirit's fruit empowered by the Holy Spirit. The counselees who have learned to produce such luscious fruit in profusion are the persons who have overcome their difficulties and might need no further counseling.

4. Adams examines the passage of 1 Corinthians 12:1-11. In doing that he explains the verses of 1-7 and the verse 11 of this passage which talks about the gifts of the Holy Spirit in general including the ministry and evangelical gifts. He overlooks the verses of 8-10 of this passage which talk specifically about the charismatic gifts of the Spirit, the concern of this study. Perhaps he believes that these gifts had ceased. They were there at the time of the apostles and the early church to validate the Gospel and since the message of the Gospel has already been established, there is no need for such gifts now.

5. However, Dye and Fee disagree with Adams regarding the cessation of the charismatic gifts recorded in 1Corinthians 12:8-10. They say that these gifts of the Holy Spirit are still available for believers today as they were at the time of the apostles. Fee comments by saying, "Those theologians who do not believe in that, have created theological positions for them that are difficult to sustain and quite removed from the biblical perspectives."

6. Fee examines the nine-fold items of the fruit of the Spirit as mentioned in Galatians 5:22-23. He says "faith" or trusting God, not "faithfulness" is meant by the Apostle Paul among the items because the latter, faithfulness, has no reference in other Paul's letters, bearing in mind that the Greek word "pistis" carries the two meanings. The list of the items is not exclusive but it is "such as." The same applies regarding the nine fold of the charismatic

gifts of 1 Corinthians 12:1-11. They are also "such as." The fruit and the charismatic gifts carry the same importance in Paul's letters.

7. Counseling Level I of Dye, or his first manual, deals with encouragement. As Crabb suggests, all members of the church should be level I counselors, in the sense that they should encourage and support other members who have problems or difficulties. According to him, this kind of counseling does not require formal training. Dye adds, the fruit of the Spirit, especially joy and peace, should be the main characters of the encouragers.

8. Counseling Level II of Dye, or his second manual, deals with Exhortation, or change in behavior in line with the Scripture. Unlike level I, the counselors should have formal training because they deal with more complex problems. His counseling model, which he adopts from Crabb, has 3 stages of Explanation, Revelation and Transformation. These stages have been explored and examined in the study.

9. Regarding the fruit and the gifts of the Spirit in his second manual, Dye does not mention the fruit of the Holy Spirit, but he highlights the charismatic gifts of the Spirit in the introduction of his second manual, especially the gifts of revelation which are the word of wisdom, the word of knowledge, and the prophesy gifts. The counselors are prompted to have these gifts and apply them in counseling, but Dye refrains from explaining how this could happen.

10. At the end of the study, I have developed a model which is based entirely on the fruit and the charismatic gifts of the Holy Spirit as well as the Scripture. I named the model, "Mustard Seed Model of Counseling." The mustard seed of faith that was been planted by the Holy Spirit in the regenerated counselee, grows by sowing to produce the fruit of the Spirit, and grows further by the filling

of the Spirit to enable the counselee to move mountains and pull up trees of problems and negative emotions, with the ultimate goal of serving and glorifying the Lord.

Finally, further studies are needed especially regarding the charismatic gifts of the Holy Spirit and their benefits in biblical counseling.

# BIBLIOGRAPHY

Adams, E Jay. *A Theology of Christian Counselling: More than Redemption.* Grand Rapids, MI: Zondervan, 1979.

Adams, E Jay. *Competent to Counsel: Introduction to Nouthetic Counselling.* Grand Rapids,MI:Zondervan,1970.

Adams, E Jay. *The Christian Counsellor's Manual: The practice of Nouthetic Counselling.* Grand Rapids, MI: Zondervan, 1973.

Adams, E Jay. "Competent to Counsel: An Interview with Jay Adams," *Talktalke Magazine* Feb.1st, 2014.

American Psychiatry Association. *Quick Reference to the Diagnostic Criteria From DSM-IV-TR.* Arlington, VA, 2000.

Baird. W. *The Corinthian Church- A Biblical Approach to Urban Culture.* New York: Abingdon,1964.

Benner D.G. *Scared Companions: The Gifts of Spiritual Friendship and Direction.* Downers Grove: Intervarsity Press,2002.

Bruce, F F. *Paul Apostle of the Heart Set Free. Grand Rapids,* MI: Eerdmans Publishing 2000.

Buddhist International Kadampa Union. *Finding Inner Peace: Meditation for Modern Life.* Flyer, Dorchester: UK, September 2015.

Carrin, Charles. *On Who's Authority?* Copies available through Charles Carrin Ministries at: www.Charles CarrinMinstries.com.

Collins English Dictionary. Glasgow, UK: HerperCollins Publishers,2006

Connors, Gerard J, Donovan, Dennis M, Diclemente, Carlo C. *Substance Abuse Treatment and the Stages of Change.* New, NY: The Guilford Press:2001.

Cook, Chris, Powell Andrew, and Sims, Andrew. *Spirituality and Psychiatry* .London, UK: Royal College of Psychiatrist Publication, 2010.

Crabb, Larry. *Basic Principles of Biblical Counselling, Meeting Counselling Needs Through The Local Church.* Grand Rapids, MI: Zondervan, 1975.

Crabb, Larry. *Effective Biblical Counselling. A Model for Helping Christians Becoming Capable Counsellors.* Grand Rapids, MI: Zondervan, 1977.

Crabb, Larry. *Inside Out.* Colorado Springs, Colorado: NavPress, 1998.

Christian Counselling Education Foundation, CCEF/UK. *Changing Hearts, Applying the Bible to Everyday Life.* London, UK: CCEF brochure, 2013.

Christian Counselling Education Foundation, CCEF/UK. *No Shame? Gospel Hope in the Experience of Shame.* London, UK: CCEF brochure,2015.

Douglas, Alban. *One Hundred Bible Lessons.* Manila, Italy: O.M.F Publishers, 1966.

Dunn, J.D.G. *Jesus, Paul and the Law.* Philadelphia, PN: Westminster publication.1999.

Dye, Colin. *Breakthrough Faith, Power in an Uncertain World.* London, UK: Hodder and Stoughton, 1995.

Dye, Colin. *Loving Obedience, Basic Biblical Counselling.* London, UK: Kensington Temple Publication,2013.

Dye, Collin. *Ministry in the Sprit, Serving in the Power of God.* London, UK: Kensington Temple Publication, 2007.

Dye, Collin. *Ministry in the Spirit, Serving in the Power of God, Student Handbook.* London, UK: Kensington Temple Publications, 2007.

Dye, Collin. *Shaped By Grace, An Introduction to Biblical Counselling.* London.UK: Kensington Temple Publication, 2012.

Eyrich, Howard, and William Hines. *Curing the Heart, A Model for Biblical Counselling.* Rose Shire, UK: Mentor Publications,2002.

Fee, D Gordon. *God's Empowering Presence, The Holy Spirit in the Letters of Paul.* Grand Rapids, MI: BakerAcademic Publications,2011.

Fee, D Gordon *Paul, the Spirit, and the People of God.* Grand Rapids, MI BakerAcademic Publications,2011.

Gill, A L. *God's Promises, For Your Every Need.* Nashville: Thomas Nelson,2008.

Green, B Joel. *Body, Soul and Human Life.* Grand Rapids,MI:BakerAcademic,2008.

Hagin, E Kenneth. *7 Vital Steps to Receiving the Holy Spirit.* Toronto, Ontario: Rhema Bible Church,1980.

Harrison, Glyn. "The New Biblical Counselling." *CMF triple helix,* London Easter Edition,2011,08.

Holy Bible, the New King James Version. Thomas Nelson Inc. 1991.

Holy Bible, Good News Bible Version .HarperCollind Publishers. 1994.

Hayford, Jack. *The Beauty of Spiritual Language, My Journey Toward the Heart of God.* Dallas: Word Publishing,1992.

Hayford, Jack. "Forward." *In HolyFire.Kendall.* R.T., Lake Mary, Florida: Charisma House,2014.

Jardine, Samuel. *The Person and Work of the Holy Spirit.* Stanton Drew, Bristol: Seed Publications,2010.

Kendall, R T. *HolyFire.* Lake Mary, Florida: Charisma House,2014.

Kendall, R T. *In Pursuit of His Wisdom.* London: Hodder and Stoughton,2014.

Kendall, R T. *The Thorn in the Flesh.* London: Hodder and Stoughton, 1999.

Lane, S Timothy. Trip, *David Paul. How People Change.* Greensboro, NC: New Growth Press.2006.

MacArthur, John and The Master's College Faculty. *Counselling, How to Counsel Biblically.* Nashville: Thomas Nelson, 2005.

Oxford English Dictionary, Paperback. Oxford, UK: Oxford University Press,2002.

Pargament, I Kenneth. *Spirituality Integrated Psychiatry, Understanding ans Addressing the Sacred.* New York, NY: The Guilford Press,2007.

Prince, Derek. *The Holy Spirit in You.* Charloote, NC: Whitaker House, 1977.

Powlison, David. *The Biblical Counselling Movement, History and Context.* Greensboro, NC:New Growth Press,2010.

Powlison, David. *Biblical Counselling in Recent Times.* Edited by John MacArthur, *Counselling, How to Counsel Biblically.* Nashville: Thomas Nelson,2005.

Pullinger, Jackie and Quicke Andrew. *Chasing the Dragon.* London, UK: Hodder &Stoughton Ltd,2001.

Riad, Youssef. *The Study of the book of Galatians.* Thru Bible,(Kolelketabe), YouTube, episode 17.

Ridderbos, Herman. *Paul, An Outline of His Theology.* Grand Rapids, MI:Eerdmans,1997.

Schaeffer, A Francis. *True Spirituality, How to Live for Jesus Moment by Moment.* Washington, DC: Tyndale House Publishers, 30th Edition, 2001.

Sherrill, John. *They Speak with Other Tongues.* Grand Rapids, MI: Chosen, a Davison of Baker Publishing Group, 40th Edition, 2004.

Sims, Andrew. *Symptoms in the Mind, An Introduction to Descriptive Psychopathology.* London, UK:W. B Saunders Company LTD,1999.

Sire, James W. *Naming the Elephant: Worldview as a Concept.* Downer Groves, IL: InterVarsity Press, 2004.

Stafford, Tim. *Personal God, Can You Really Know the One Who Made the Universe.* Grand Rapids, MI:Zondervan, 2008.

Subritzky, Bill. *Explaining The Anointing of God*. Kent, England: Sovereign World Limited, 1991.

Virkler, Mark, and Patti Virkler. Counselled By God, Emotional Wholeness by Hearing God's Voice. Shippensburg, PA: Destiny Image Publishers, 1989.

Waters, Jen. "Speaking in Tongues." *Washington Times*, The (DC). 01/11/2005.

Welch, Edward T. Are You Feeling Inadequate? A Letter to Biblical Counsellors." *The Journal of Biblical Counselling*: CCEF, Volume 26.number 3, 2012.

Worthington Jr, Everett L. *Hope-Focused Marriage Counselling, A Guide to Brief Therapy*. Downers Grove, IL: InterVarsity Press,1999.

Youssef Ibrahim. "Spirituality and Psychiatry." Paper presented at the monthly psychiatrists' meeting, Dorchester, UK, February 12, 2013.

Printed in the United States
By Bookmasters